Process
for
Purpose

Volume I

Stephanie Arrington

ISBN 978-1-68570-754-5 (paperback)
ISBN 978-1-68570-755-2 (digital)

Christian Faith Publishing
832 Park Avenue
Meadville, PA 16335
www.christianfaithpublishing.com

Printed in the United States of America

In loving memory of my daddy,
Lawrence Dow Jr.

Dedication

To my mother, my ladybug, whom I love dearly, thank you for giving me life. Most of all, I thank you for your prayers.

To Jay, my son, because of you, I am who I am in more ways than you can imagine. You are a living testimony that God can and will deliver. I love you, and great things are yet to be seen. Look closely at your life. Nobody did it but God.

To Johnet, my daughter, you being born saved my life many times than you can imagine. You are one of the most gifted, talented, smart, compassionate, and loving living being I know. You are growing up to be a beautiful young woman. God has blessed you as a seer and with a prophetic gift to sing, write music, and play the piano for his glory and to bring deliverance to the lives of many for such a time as this.

Contents

Foreword

In our quest to discover our purpose in life, it can be a wandering winding road of the unknown. Fortunately for us, God does not leave us without His plan already in place, even if He does not reveal it to us when we want Him to. The road to your purpose and destiny is a journey you will not soon forget or even want to. In her book, *Process for Purpose*, Stephanie Arrington gives us insight to deliverance as the tool God gives us to help understand our walk with the Lord and how it is necessary for us to go through it to lead to a clear path into our purpose and destiny. The journey of her personal experience and transparency will leave you wanting more of God with clarity about your purpose than ever before. This book will encourage you to dig in deep with your foundation of purpose through deliverance to help you grow in your relationship with the Lord and cause you to go after your purpose and destiny with zeal and knowledge. Proverbs 4:7 tells us, *"Wisdom is the principal thing; therefore get wisdom: and in all of thy getting get understanding."* This is the road we all want to travel successfully, and this book will help you do just that. Get ready for your life to change and the progress that you make will be amazing!

—Darryl Chavers, Sr., Presiding Apostle
Purpose & Destiny International Network

Acknowledgments

I would like to take the time to acknowledge those that help make this book possible. I give thanks first to God for calling me to be a prophet for such a time as this and using my mother's womb as an incubator to form me into purpose.

I thank God for the late Apostle William Brown, founder of Salvation and Deliverance Churches Worldwide, where my life of prayer and fasting was birthed out of me and where I was taught the importance of spiritual discernment and living a life of holiness.

I want to thank my daughter, Johnet, for when I didn't have a title for my book, you prayed and God gave you a title. So it was with you that the Lord spoke in a dream that this book found purpose and was made complete.

I thank God for the late Bishop Walter E. Holmes, God's apostolic gift, for speaking into my life on May 6, 2011, confirming the writing of this book and many volumes to follow. Those same prophetic words I penned in my journal. Every time I struggled with writing this book or was under great attack from the enemy, I would go back and read those words. Thank you, because that word pushed me beyond limitations to complete this task.

I thank you, Bishop Keith Wright Sr., for making yourself available to my family throughout the years since my son was a little boy. You told me that this book will bring deliverance to many and their lives will be changed. I want to let you know I appreciate you and I am grateful for your prayers and encouraging words.

To Prophet Gerald Armstrong, my brother and friend, you have been there when no one else seemed to be available. Man of God, you have contributed to my family in ways no one else knows of. You were there not just for me but also for my children, Jay and Johnet. Thank you for your prayers and just being there. I love you.

To Minister Michael Hailstock, God's prophet, my brother and friend. You have prayed me through many times when I couldn't pray, I felt like I was losing my mind, and all I could do was cry. In the middle of the night, when I called for someone to pray for me and couldn't get through to anybody, I got through to you. I love you in all sincerity.

To Minister Marlo Ingram, the friend that will always be tucked away in heart, you are truly a woman of prayer and substance. And there is much more to be birthed out. We have so much history together. You play a special part in this book being birthed out of me in more ways than you may know. We have prayed together, and we have fasted together. We laughed together, and we cried together. We shopped together, and we prepared meals together. We went through together. My lord, the trials we went through back then, but thank God for his continued deliverance. I never forgot the little things that made the big difference. I love you not just as a friend but also as a sister.

To Angela Cowan, God's prophetic intercessor and prophetic vessel, I thank God for reconnecting us years ago at The Threshing Floor. Thank you for your *"suddenly"* prayers when we were on the phone. Prayer has always been the foundation of your ministry. I can remember you telling me, when I was struggling with my writing, to set aside a time each day to write for at least one or two hours. It's truly the little things that make a big difference.

Introduction

What is a process? What does it mean to go through a process? For many, it can mean a number of things. For example, most people have to go through certain procedures to start working on a new job or, better yet, go back to school to even qualify for the job. So what does being "processed" mean for a Christian? When it comes to doing service for God, we go through a process of preparation. Depending on our submission to the Holy Spirit, some processes will take longer than others. We must go through a process so that we may qualify for the task that God has for us. We have to be equipped for the job. This process can at times be very painful because we are confronted with issues that we didn't have to or want to deal with. We, as human beings, become uncomfortable with change because we are so used to doing things a particular way that even an invitation to change will begin the process of dealing with feelings we don't want to deal with. As human beings, we become accustomed to our environment. Our environment plays a major role in how we see ourselves. It can impact the way we think, feel, view others, and embrace or reject the world around us. Most of all, it can impact how we deal with and resolve certain issues in our life.

When we come into relationship with Christ, we are like newborn babes entering into a new world. We have to be retrained and retaught. What needs to be taught and how receptive we are will, in part, depend on our past experiences. The body of Christ consists of a spectrum of people and their past experiences. Some have been rejected, abused, homeless, drug users, etc., while others never experienced any of these setbacks. Still there are others who think because they have a great job and a fancy car and are very educated that they have it altogether. Still in all, many that feel this way live lonely lives and are miserable because they feel things will fill the void in their lives. In this book, I will use my life story as an example of what it means to go through a spiritual process. My process may be totally different from the things you had to endure, but it was still *your* process.

When I look back over my life, I realize I could not have been brought from the womb unless there was a purpose for my life. My life was predestined; God had a set time and date that I would be conceived. With that conception came my destiny. With my destiny came my aspirations. With my aspirations came the decision to be what God called me to be. We all have a purpose, and if we don't know what our purpose is, we will live a life of not feeling any sense of fulfillment. I don't understand a lot of the times why I feel the way that I do. Most of the time, it is not something I can attach a sound reason. My birth was not one of random selection but one that gave life to the question, but why God? You may be wondering why I question God giving me life. Well, for starters, I lived most of my life wanting to die. I often asked why I had to go through all that I had to go through. Today, I realize it was to bring me to the place that I am now.

As I move forward in writing, as you read, many sections of this book may appear to be repetitive. What we must understand is that many events in our life may have a tendency to repeat themselves if we fail to change or attempt to make an effort in changing our circumstances. At times, this change calls for repeated and continuous deliverance in our lives that is part of our process. This is so we can get to the place that God has designed and prepared for us. Therefore, to repeat verbatim specific circumstances, scripture, etc., is to be able to target a particular spirit so that the deliverance process can begin in your life. Let the Lord have his way in you as you go on your journey to deliverance. Remember, it's a process! So I ask that you recognize your need for deliverance and allow the transforming work of God to continue in your life.

Why Me, Lord?

And we know that all things work together for good to them that
love God, to them who are the called according to his purpose.
—Romans 8:28, KJV

For many years, I struggled with accepting the call and, in turn, wanting to be accepted by others. Now this would take me back as far as my childhood. I had a very difficult life growing up as a child. I resorted to drugs at an early age, suffered from severe depression that led to my first suicide attempt at age fourteen as many others followed way into my young adult years. I was in and out of mental institution with many coming to the conclusion that I was a lost cause. Well, so I thought. All these life-altering experiences resulted from rejection, low self-esteem, emotional and verbal and psychological abuse, being sexually violated from a young age, and the list can go on. I became very familiar with struggles, defeat, suffering, rejection, loneliness, and hardship during and beyond the early years in my life. I realize that God had a purpose in mind for me, and that purpose would form my destiny as I go through the process of deliverance, answer the call, and take my rightful place in Christ. I now know that "Before *He* formed *me* in the belly *He* knew *me*; and before *I came* forth out of the womb *He* sanctified *me* and ordained *me* a prophet unto the nations" (Jeremiah 1:5, emphasis mine). The amplified version says, "Before I formed you in the womb I knew [and] approved of you [as my chosen instrument], and before you were born I separated and set you apart, consecrating you; [and] I appointed you as a prophet to the nations" (Jeremiah 1:5, AMP).

I can remember the time when I went to a revival service at a former pastor's church many years ago; he ministered to me and said there is a prophet in the building. He then came to me and said, "This is the anointing that is on your life." To be honest, I had no clue what the term *prophet* meant, let alone *called*. My godmother, who was an evangelist at that time, explained to me what a prophet was, and I began to study the topic and character of a prophet myself and get answers through my research, study and thereafter began to have personal experiences with the Holy Spirit (2 Timothy 2:15; 1 John 2:27). The Lord also began to use me in the gift of prophecy, intercessory prayer, and spiritual warfare as a prayer warrior. My passion and desire to pray, fast, and study the Word of God became more intense. In the past, I have had two out of body experiences and literally heard the audible voice of God once. I never heard the Lord speak to me the way he spoke to me on that day again. The experience was as if someone was in the same room talking to me. Dreams and visions became more consistent and often. Then I began to understand that it is just more than standing in an office; it is the processing you have to go through to get there. The office is not one you just walk into overnight, but it takes years of preparation. The more dynamic the call, the more fiery and intense the severing process is. The process that I experienced and still am experiencing is God "killing me." I have to die to the flesh. No, I am not having the same experiences, and God is not using me in the same capacity as he has before, but it seems like I am going through more trials and suffering than anything else. But one thing I have come to realize is that our trials are part of the process, the part that we need to be delivered from, things that are hidden and things we may not have realized were there until God revealed it to us, and the part that God has to show us how messed up we are. Nevertheless, to God be the glory, because it is all part of the process, my process, and I have said yes to the call. It is a painful process, but I am in a place where I just want to please God and do what he called me to do. God wants clean, consecrated vessels to be used for his glory. So in writing this book, I hope to encourage, strengthen, and build up others to know that if God called you and you are a part of the remnant, he will be with you through your process, and in the end, you will come forth as pure gold (Zechariah 13:9, NLT). Don't give up or give in, because God is a rewarder to them that diligently seek him and believe that the best is yet to come (Hebrews 11:6)!

For the Glory of God

*And the glory of God shall be revealed, and all flesh shall see
it together: for the mouth of the Lord hath spoken it.*
—Isaiah 40:5, KJV

When the Lord had ministered to me about writing this book, it
wasn't writing the book that was difficult, but it was telling my story
that was. It took me five years to write this book. I was ashamed
of the person I was and the things that I did. Starting this book
about the life I once lived and testifying of some of the things I went
through as a Christian is enough to know that there would be a spiritual battle, a battle of the mind. Who wants to revisit those places
you truly believe you were delivered from but come to realize there
was still some residue left behind? I was one of those people. I have
been wrestling with this book for several years now, but in order to be
fully delivered, go to another phase of my purification process, and
move forward toward my destiny, I must do what God has charged
me to do. This book, *Process for Purpose*, is to minister to someone
who is in need of deliverance to let them know that God can and will
deliver and of a testimony of what God did and is still doing in my
life. It is for the glory of God.

So beloved, I intended for this book not to draw attention to
me but to draw your attention toward God and allow you to see how
big God is and that he can do all things but fail (Luke 1:37).

I always had a desire and still do have a great desire to be used
by the Lord in an extraordinary way and, most of all, to have a close,
intimate relationship with the Lord and be in a place where my life

will minister to others. So my prayer is that the words of these pages will touch the heart of someone who may have doubted or given up on God to come to see that God can do what others may deem impossible.

This book will make full proof of the ministry that God has called me to—not just to walk in the office of the prophet, but to touch and change lives because of Christ and the spirit of God that lives in me. This book will not just bring deliverance to others who have gone through or are still going through similar situations, but I know that as I write this book and revisit my past, I too will go through a deliverance process and I will be forever changed.

The Past

Brethren, I count not myself to have apprehended, but this one thing I do, forgetting those things which are behind, and reaching forth unto those things which are before.
—Phil 3:13, KJV

As a young child, I always felt that I had to please others. I had to have the perfect grade, the perfect clothes; everything had to be just right, but my life was far from perfect. I started experimenting with drugs at a very young age. I can remember a family member giving me an LSD tab of paper to put on my tongue at a movie theater we sneaked into. (Today I know that it was because of the side effects I was having.) I began hallucinating, and my perception was off. That day was just a foretaste of what I would become addicted to. I was introduced to marijuana, and soon after that, I began to lace it with cocaine. I sniffed heroine before, but my drug of choice eventually became crack cocaine. I very rarely was able to freebase with pure cocaine unless someone else was buying it or I was an invited guest, and believe me, it was not always free. I sold my body for crack cocaine on several occasions when I didn't have any money to buy more.

From the age of fourteen, I suffered from severe cases of rejection, which led to deep depression, which led to many suicide attempts, which led to many mental institutions. The first time I tried to take my life was at age fourteen, and God miraculously put life back into my body. From my sister's and mother's testimony of what was happening when I was in an unconscious state, I was vomiting and defecating at the same time, and my heart went into a supraventricular tachycardia state. My sister said that my heart appeared as if it were coming out of my chest. The state that I was in was too unbearable to watch, so my mother and sister had to leave the room. The doctors said there was no more they could do for me, and they just had to wait and see if I would come to.

From that point on, I experienced numerous suicide attempts, states of severe depression, and being in and out of psychiatric hospitals and mental institutions. I developed a low self-esteem and became rebellious against my mother, who was very strict. I sneaked around to be with guys, and of course, I started having sex at a very young age without protection, which later on led to several pregnancies and abortions. I even was intimate with someone who had AIDS, which I didn't find out until he died. I was manipulated at a very young age to engage in sexual activity with a family member. It was incest. This same spirit manifested when I was under the influence of drugs. It was this same family member I let fondle my body just for a high. When I got saved, I confronted them, and they denied ever touching me. I am sorry if I am being too transparent, but even after I got saved, I still battled that demon in my mind; the enemy would taunt me time and time again until God delivered me. My deliverance came through much prayer and fasting.

Rejection caused a lot of pain in my life. Being hurt and rejected by men led me to try to find acceptance in another lifestyle. Little did I know, I would just experience more pain and that void would never be filled until I surrendered my life to the Lord. I thank God for his grace and mercy on my life. Even in these relationships, God was pulling at me, but I would not surrender. It was not until I decided enough was enough. It wasn't until I got tired of going through the same cycle of pain, rejection, and suicidal attempts that I decided to go back to church, and I had already purposed in my heart that that day would be my day of salvation. I will never forget that the former Apostle William Brown preached the message "Your Secret Is Out." I felt like God had showed him everything about my life and he was preaching to me. It was a message from God, because when the altar call was made, I was the first one to get up from my seat. I lived in a backslid state for many years, and believe me, I made my life harder than it should have been. To let some of you who are outside the will of God know, don't wait until you think you can get it together to come back to God; that's his job. God is a loving and merciful God, but the spirit will not always strive with man (Genesis 6:3).

There are things I still at times battle in my mind, but if I want to move forward in what God has for me, I have to be free in every area of my life. Our minds have to be renewed by the washing of water by the Word. The mind is a part of the soul, along with the will and emotions, so there is always a battle going on. Therefore, we have to go through a cleansing process by washing with the Word of God. We have to come to a place in our lives where we must realize that whatever we do, it has to please God. So many of us are in church and have been for years, and we lived with situations that have not been confronted. We hide them behind our shout, we preach them in our message, and some of us even wear them because of the way we dress. But deep down inside, we are wrestling with a spirit of denial and we say, "I'm all right." Some even hide behind their titles and live false lives and are not delivered. So when they minister to others, that person can't be set free because the person ministering is still in bondage. How can someone who is not free bring deliverance to someone who needs to be free? In order to preach deliverance, we have to be delivered, live in and maintain our deliverance. Our mission in this life is to have such an impact on others that it leaves an impression. There are certain conditions that go along with being delivered. First, you have to want to be delivered. Making a confession of the things you need to be delivered from can be a step toward deliverance, allowing God to begin the process of deliverance. You must be in constant prayer and his Word. Some yokes can only be broken off your life through fasting. So some things may require that you commit yourself to prayer and fasting for an extended length of time. There were times I had to fast in order for me to be delivered from some things that had me in bondage. Now I have made prayer and fasting a part of my lifestyle.

A Spirit Called Depression

I have told you these things, so that in me you may have peace.
In this world you will have trouble. But take
heart! I have overcome the world.
—John 16:33, NIV

This is a spirit that I experienced many days in my lifetime. Depression will make you feel helpless and, most of all, empty. Sometimes I would cry all the time because I felt like no one understood me or cared. I had people in my life that tried to comfort me and tell me that whatever it was, I was going to be okay. They did not understand that I didn't want to be okay; I just wanted to be dead.

Depression is a spirit that gets hold of you, and it literally feels like all life is being sucked out of you to the point where all you feel is never-ending pain. If you know the characteristics of the python snake, it literally feels like the life is being sucked out of you. If you know anything about the python, then you would know that it is not a venomous snake and it will not attack you unless provoked or stressed. So in other words, if there is an open door (depression) for the enemy to feed off, he will sit in the seat of your soul until all the life (spirit) has left you—your will to live. It is a pain so deep that you will come to believe that the only way it can stop is to die. That is a lie, but that is what the enemy wants us to believe. The Word of God tells us in John 8:44:

> *You are of your father the devil, and the lusts*
> *of your father ye will do. He was a murderer from*

the beginning and abode not in the truth, because
there is not truth in him. When he speaketh a lie, he
speaketh of his own: for he is a liar, and the father
of it.

According to the *American Heritage College Dictionary,* depression is a condition of feeling sad or despondent. If looked at from a psychological point of view, it can be defined or characterized as a psychological disorder given into the inability to concentrate, insomnia, loss of appetite, and feelings of extreme sadness, dejection, and hopelessness. From a spiritual perspective, when we look at the affliction, it is considered a condition of the body, soul, or spirit. So from the mental and/or psychological perspective, depression is one of the manifestations or symptoms of the spirit of affliction. Affliction can cause physical or mental stress. The Hebrew word for *affliction* is *oniy,* which means depression, and *ra,* which means bad or evil. So when we focus on the spiritual dimensions of depression, we can see that it is a spirit that has only one purpose, and that is to control or take over the total person.

Growing up as a child, as far back as I can remember, my goal was always to please others or make others happy. So when I failed at that, I felt like I would never amount to nothing or be a person of value. Well, that is also what I was told most of the time, especially when I was told that I "wasn't going to be anything" by the people that are supposed to love me but just don't know how to express that love. At that point, I began to believe it and then live it out. I would think in my mind that if the next time I tried to kill myself, I was successful at doing it, maybe, just maybe someone will then feel and understand the pain that I felt when I was alive. Coming to the point where your only desire is to die is getting to the point of feeling like there is no return once you are there. I felt like there was no need to live. My will even felt like it had died in me. I would always be contemplating in my mind how I could try to kill myself again and again and again. Each time I tried, the hand of God was there to pull me back. I can't even begin to count the times I tried to take my life. There were times I took pills, went to sleep, but woke up the next day. I can recall a time when I was so depressed and the feeling of "I can't take it anymore" came over me, and that night, I decided to go to the roof of my building and jump off. I stood on the edge of the roof, crying and saying, "God, help me. I can't take it anymore," and at that moment, it was as if something pulled me away from the edge. Another time was when the devil was talking to me and telling me, "You should try hanging yourself, because you took pills, but that didn't work." I just wanted to stop hearing the voices that were talking in my ear. I was in the kitchen; I covered my ears, trying to stop the voices, and at that moment, I got a knife and began to cut both of my wrists. I actually felt like something, some sort of force, was pulling me to do these things. I went and lay on the bed until I went to sleep. They had to come up the fire escape and break the window to get in my apartment where they found me in the bed. It was not my time. God has a purpose for my life that must be fulfilled.

For I know the thoughts that I think towards you, saith the Lord, thoughts of peace, and not of evil, to give you an expected end. (Jeremiah 29:11)

God created us and placed his purpose within us to do his will. We can either do his will or go after our own will. Today, I know his will is right and perfect. There is a way that seems right to a man, but the end thereof is the ways of death (Proverbs 14:12). So we have a choice: to follow God or to be led by the wisdom of this world. From my own experiences, I found that when we rebel against the call of God and go our pernicious ways, we have to suffer the consequences. In other words, we reap what we sow (Galatians 6:7). We can choose life, or we can choose death, and we can only find life in Christ (Romans 8:12). I was like a dead woman walking. I had no direction in my life and no clue to where I was going to end up being. All I knew was that I was tired of feeling the same way day in and day out. So I tried the way of death.

Depression becomes and is a battle that takes place in the mind constantly. I literally would hear voices telling me I was never going to be anything and anything else that could sap more life out of me, what I had left. When a lot of bad things happen to you in life and, as a child, you are told negative things, those things begin to shape your life if you allow them to.

I can remember times when I ministered to others and I needed to be ministered to. I was a prayer warrior for six years. Praying, fasting, and studying the Word of God became my lifestyle. I never missed a service, and I never missed a prayer meeting, but I fell into the sin of fornication and had a child. I want to remind you that the devil will have you thinking that a one-month thrill is going to end up as a lifetime commitment. I was deceived by the devil, even though I was hearing from God and he was using me. I put my guard down, so a self-righteous spirit had set in. You have to be careful of passing judgment over someone you feel does not match up to your standards. Self-righteousness is a religious spirit. When we have a religious spirit, we become judgmental and critical and think we are in a place with God that no one else is (false holiness). I was doing all the right things, but was I really allowing God to do the rights things in me and through me.

I write this book out of obedience, not for any personal gain or recognition. This book was birthed out of my spirit. Now I trust God to guide my hand and give me divine instruction on what to write. I can't pick and choose what I want to write because I feel I don't want people to know who I once was. So I have to depend solely on the Holy Spirit to be my counselor and to cover me in the blood. I believe and know without a shadow of a doubt that God would not give me this assignment without covering me.

Suicide and Pride

"Be not over much wicked, neither be thou foolish:
why shouldest thou die before thy time?"
—Ecclesiastes 7:17, ASV

The Center of Disease Control and Prevention published a study on the impact of economy on suicidal rates in the United States and found that the increase and decline in incidents happen in conjunction with the flux of national economy. The main finding is significantly linked between business cycles and suicide among those of working ages twenty-five to sixty-five. Studies are built on historical facts that statistically state that overall suicide rates soared during recession periods such as the Great Depression (1929–1933). There are many other factors that confirm the increase of suicidal rates and its link to recession, collapse, or crisis, with the Great Depression having the highest suicide rate and increase to an overall high for the longest period in history. Today, there are many resources that people tend to seek out to prevent suicide. There are crisis centers, support groups, counselors, and mental health care systems, to name a few. Others may reach out to family members and churches for help.

Natural Diagnosis versus Spiritual Prognosis

One may ask, "What is the root cause of a person wanting to commit suicide?" Myself being someone who battled suicide, was in and out of mental institutions, and even faced death when the doctors said there was no more they could do, I can only share what I have experienced and have been delivered from.

Suicide is defined as intentionally taking one's life—in other words, murdering oneself, which is plainly acting against the commandment of God "Thou shalt not kill" (Exodus 20:4). Prior to the late-nineteenth century, suicide was legally defined as a criminal act in most Western countries. In the social climate of the early 2000s, however, suicidal behavior is most commonly regarded and responded to as a psychiatric "emergency." Suicide has become a major public health problem as well as a personal tragedy.

When faced with overwhelming depression, feelings of rejection, low self-esteem, abuse (whether it is verbal, emotional, psychological, or physical), rape, incest, and other victimizing acts, one can become emotionally distraught to the point where one feels life is not worth living anymore. Some have been so devastated by life tragedies and circumstances that they have allowed them to take control of their entire being where they are no more mentally stable. At this point, those individuals may have to be medicated and even spend the rest of their lives in an insane asylum.

Now looking at suicide from a spiritual perspective, we will see that suicide is a manifestation of a spirit itself. The deaf and dumb spirit is often assigned to children (Mark 9:17–27), and it acts as a door to other spirits. Here, we see suicide as being a demonic influence and can drive a person to take his own life, which is contrary to the will of God and is originated in the realm of the demonic host (John 10:10). In this incidence, we can look at murder or suicide as being a pardonable sin. The Bible speaks of the only unforgivable sin as rejecting Christ (Mark 16:16) and blasphemy against the Holy Spirit (Mark 3:28–29). This is why we, as Christians, must be born again of the water and of the Spirit and be transformed by the renewing of our minds (John 3:5, Romans 12:2). This is not a "one-shot deal"; we have to seek the face of God, guard our hearts and spirit, fast and pray, study and meditate on the Word of God in order to maintain a consistent relationship and closeness with God. The Bible also speaks of great people who became overwhelmed with grief to the point they wished they had never been born: Elijah (1 Kings

19:4), Jeremiah (Jeremiah 20:14–18), Job (Job 3:1–3; 7:15–16), Jonah (Jonah 4:8). The spirit of fear is another spirit where suicide can be manifested. Acts 16:27–28 speaks of when the keeper of the prison drew his sword to kill himself because he thought that the prisoners were gone, but Paul intervened and told him to do no harm to himself. Fear comes from the root word *pholoos*, meaning to cause to take flight. It is a psychological reaction to something or someone who poses a threat to our sense of security and safety. Fear has so much depth that it is experienced not only by an individual but nationally as well (Deuteronomy 2:25).

If I want to touch on spiritual suicide, I would first have to define what each word means. *Spiritual* is defined as whatever pertains to the immaterial and invisible spheres of God's creation (Hosea 9:7; 1 Corinthians 2:15 and 15:44–46). So that would define *spiritual suicide* as an act that would cause the human soul to lose its connection and intimate communion with God. In other words, the believer has become fleshly and carnal. The believer has given up the right for the Holy Spirit to dominate. The soul of the believer is no longer governed by the spirit of God. Even though there are many ways an individual can commit spiritual suicide, I am going to focus on one spirit because it has many signs and manifestations. A spirit that can cause spiritual suicide is the spirit of divination, because this spirit is responsible for straight-out, blatant rebellion and no submission to authority. Some of the signs and manifestations of this spirit are, but not limited to, control, discouragement, depression, deception, perversion, suspicions, idolatry, superstition, false prophets, familiar spirits, etc. The spirit of rebellion is the foundation on • which Satan's kingdom of darkness is built (Isaiah 14:12–15). The principality of the spirit of divination counterfeits the work of the Holy Spirit (Deuteronomy 18:10–12, Acts 16:16). Spiritual suicide can cause a believer to become "spiritually bankrupt" because of disobedience, wavering faith, unrighteousness, and sin. We must make it a daily habit to attend to our spiritual needs by prayer, fasting, seeking God, learning the strategies of spiritual warfare, and diligently studying the Word of God.

Pride

*Now I Nebuchadnezzar praise and extol and honor the King
of heaven, all whose works are truth, and his ways judgment,
and those that walk in pride he is able to abase.*
—Daniel 4:37, KJV

The Hebrew word for *pride* is *ge'ah* (pronounced "gay-aw"), which
means arrogance. Pride can be negative or positive, depending on
what manner it is used. Pride can be described as having a sense of
one's own dignity or value and self-respect. Paul expressed justifiable
pride in his fellowship with the Philippians (Phil. 1:3–6). It can also
be described as being arrogant, conceited, haughty, and full of vanity
(this is excessive pride in one's appearance or accomplishments). This
type of pride will result in self-righteousness (Luke 18:11–12, the
Pharisee and the publican) and self-deception (Jeremiah 49:16; the
downfall of the Edomites was their pride, which made them overly
confident). Most of the time, pride is used as one of Satan's weapons in the life of the believer. The Word of God tells us that "when
pride cometh, then cometh shame: but with the lowly is wisdom"
(Proverbs 11:2) and "pride goeth before destruction, and a haughty
spirit before a fall" (Proverbs 16:18). Few of us as Christians fail to
admit ever being confronted with pride, and some still battle with a
spirit of pride even after being delivered. We are to repent when we
recognize pride rising in us and trying to take root. Pride can cause
a person not to have favor with God and not prosper in ministry.
Though this may be a major common factor in the body of Christ,
a lot of people will not admit to having pride or ever experiencing

it, and a lot of people seem not to repent. Pride can be so subtle that it can be very hard to detect its manifestations; therefore, many of us cannot notice the signs of pride. Some of the signs of pride are as follows:

1. Insecurity but there is security in God (Deuteronomy 31:8)
2. The need to be right (Romans 13:1, NLT)
3. Being argumentative (James 4:1–3)
4. Anger (Ecclesiastes 7:9)
5. Not easily corrected (Titus 2:15)
6. Needing to proclaim our titles or degrees when we are to be servants of the Lord (Romans 6:22)
7. The need to compare ourselves to others and having a spirit of competition (2 Corinthians 10:12, NLT)

Now I am not concurring that if you have one of these manifestations, you have a spirit of pride. But what we have to realize and be aware of is our need for deliverance and that this need is continuous.

We, as children of God, have to be so careful not to allow pride to become a snare in our life. First John 2:16 says, "For all that is in the world, the lust of the flesh, and the lust of the eyes, and the pride of life, is not of the Father, but is of the world." It is okay to have nice clothes, a beautiful home, and an expensive car if these are what God has blessed you with, but when we lust for them, they become a snare and can develop pride in us.

Many of us have spiritual gifts to be used for the glory of God and the edifying and building up of the church. If they are used for the wrong purpose and we don't give these gifts back to God, pride can take over, and then you are no longer operating under the guidance and the unction of the Holy Spirit but under the power of Satan and your gift has become false. These gifts are of the flesh and will not bring peace and joy in Christ or repentance and a closer fellowship with Christ.

Satan used his weapon of pride in the life of David. After David had many triumphant victories, Satan enticed him with pride by numbering the people (1 Chronicles 18–20; 21:1–6). This was a sin of the flesh. Here we can see that when a person is successful and given much, the spiritual battle against pride becomes intense. We are to give God all glory for all he does in us and through us! Satan is very skillful in inflating pride in us, and that is why we have to always be prayerful and watchful, have keen spiritual discernment, and know the tactics of the enemy (1 Peter 4:7, Hebrews 5:14, 1 Peter 5:8). We have to also be careful not to allow people to "glorify" us instead of giving God the glory. Peter tells us, "Be clothed with humility: for God resisteth the proud, and giveth grace to the humble. Humble yourselves therefore under the mighty hand of God, that he may exalt you in due time" (First Peter 5:5,6). This clearly shows that humility is an indication of our dependence on God and recognizing that all we achieve and accomplish is because of the grace of God. Jesus showed humility when "he riseth from supper, and laid aside his garments, and took a towel and girded himself. After that he poureth water into a bason, and began to wash the disciples' feet and to wipe them with the towel wherewith he was girded" (John 13:4,5).

The spirit of pride is the very foundation with which Satan has built his kingdom. This spirit's origin finds its way into the very heart of Satan. Pride is a protector of self. It does not betray self, expose self, or tell on self because it is obsessed with self. Ezekiel 28:13–19 describes this pride by portraying it in the prince of Tyrus, giving us a veiled description of Satan. He was an anointed cherub (verse 14) and perfect creature in all his ways until iniquity was found in him (verse 15), and his heart became lifted up, and he was driven out before the presence of God (verse 17). Some of the signs of pride that Satan had were rebellion, self-importance, disobedience, selfishness, and deception. If and when we see any of these manifestations in our lives, we must go to God, repent, begin to war in the spirit and release true humility, call those things that are not as though they were, activate our faith in God to deliver us, and not allow the spirit of pride to get a foothold in our lives.

Prayer of Deliverance from the Spirit of Pride

Father God, in the name of Jesus, I come to you with a repentant heart, asking you, Lord, to forgive me for the times I allowed pride to manifest in my life. I ask that you will continue to keep me on the potter's wheel that I may grow in the grace of God and be all that you called me to be according to your will, purpose, and plan for my life. I pray that anytime that pride tries to come in, a spirit of conviction will fall on me to correct me and thereby change me. My desire, God, is to please you. So, Father, I humbly submit my will, my ways, and my intents to you. I give back to you every gift that you may purify and refine them as you do work in me, that whatever I do and say would be for your glory, God. I release true humility in my life, submission to your will and ways, repentance, a spirit of giving, and faith. Birth in and out of me the fruit of the spirit, because your Word says to seek ye first the kingdom of God and all his righteousness and all these things shall be added unto me. Today, I deny myself. Crucify my flesh that I will die daily to self. I bind every spirit, plan, and plot of the enemy that tries to hinder the work that you are doing in me, and I release the anointing of God over my life right now in Jesus's name. Amen.

The Dream

*Then was the secret revealed unto Daniel in a vision of
the night. Then Daniel blessed the God of heaven.*
—Daniel 2:19, ASV

On October 26, 2008, I was lying in bed, just resting. It was day-
time, and I began to drift off and dream. Well, I believe it was a
dream. In the dream, I was at Barnes and Noble and asked the man
at the counter, "How do I begin to write a book?" because I need to
start on my book. I began to tell him that I have a bachelor's degree
and master's degree, but he told me that anyone can write a book.
In other words, he was saying your degrees mean nothing to God.
If he gives you an assignment, he will equip you to do it. Then a
young lady began to look through a list of names in a book to see if
my name was in it, but she said she couldn't find it. So I began to
look through the list myself and found my name two times on two
different pages. Then the man brought me a book and opened it.
The title of the book read *For the Glory of God*; the dedication page
read "To my mother, whom I love dearly." Thereafter, he began to
talk to me about the table of contents and foreword pages. In my
dream, I began to revisit my past. When I opened my eyes, I was
crying, and the power of God was on me very heavily. I lay there on
the bed and began to tell God yes. I began praying in my heavenly
language, and as I was praying, the spirit of the Lord was giving me
instructions: "Cover yourself in prayer and fasting, because as you
are writing this book, the enemy will attack you, you will experience

your past again and cover your mind in the blood of Jesus. This book will be a testimony.

As I tried to get out of bed to go to my prayer room, the power of God was still upon me; I fell prostrate on my face before the Lord. And the spirit of the Lord said, "Even now I am changing your appetite, and it will be for more of the things of me."

The First Confirmation

But seek ye first the kingdom of God and His righteousness,
and all these things shall be added unto you.
—Matthew 6:33, KJV

I was going through very intense warfare, especially in my mind, but God used a woman of God to pray and minister to me over the phone. That night, I got a breakthrough, and then came the confirmation. She began to tell me there was a book that the Lord wanted me to write. Again, I put the pen to the paper, but to no avail, I retired from the assignment once again. I decided to go back to school to get another master's degree. In my mind, I was thinking this would change my current situation and more job opportunities would be available to me. First of all, I didn't seek God about this to see if this was what he wanted me to do in that season. I never completed the program. I had one more class to complete in order to graduate but was not able to pay the tuition. One thing I learned is, when we try to obtain things without God's guidance or assistance, we will fail. We have to put him first in whatever we strive to do (Matthew 6:33). We have to make sure it is the assignment that he has for us in that season.

I Trust You, Lord

When I am afraid, I put my trust in you.
—Psalms 56:3, NIV

"I trust you, Lord"—these were the words I continued to say through every heartache, through every tear, through every disappointment, and when I couldn't say anything else. These few words of prayer when I couldn't pray brought me through many trials and great tribulation.

It all began in the year 1998 when I decided to pick up my cross and follow Christ. I was truly tried in the fire. The enemy began to attack the one person that was closest to me, my son. He stopped going to school. If I can remember, I believe he only went as far as the eighth or ninth grade, if he even completed that. He started using drugs, got caught up in the streets and only God knows what else. Prison became his second home apart from the streets. It seemed like the more I prayed and fasted, the worse things got.

I remember the times when I didn't have a clue as to where my son was for days because I rarely saw him. I would pray and ask God to just watch over him and keep him covered in his blood. I can recall one New Year's Eve (prior to that, I hadn't heard from my son in about three days) when I prayed and asked the Lord to give me a sign that he was okay. That night, he called to tell me he was coming home later. He sounded like he was high on drugs and had been drinking, but he never came home that night. But I thank God that he allowed my son to call me to let me know he was still alive. With all the times that he had left home for days, the fear of getting a phone call saying that my son was dead haunted me many nights.

Many days and nights went by when I didn't see my son, but I continued to trust God. I continued to intercede on his behalf. I remember so clearly, as if it happened just yesterday, the Holy Spirit waking me up around 10:00 or 11:00 p.m. one night and, as plain as I was writing it, telling me to begin to intercede for my son. I sat up in bed and began to pray, but the Holy Spirit unctioned me to get on my face and lie prostrate as I pray. After following the instruction of the Holy Spirit, I felt an unusual uneasiness in my spirit in which I could not find rest. So I decided to call my sister to see if my son had been to her home, and she informed me that her son and mine had come there earlier and they both were under the influence of drugs. Sometime after midnight, I received a call from the precinct, and an officer was telling me my son had been arrested. I asked if I could speak to him but was told he could call me on his free call. When I finally spoke to him, it was confirmed that the time the Holy Spirit woke me up was the same time he was arrested. The cops had chased him on the subway platform, threw him down to the ground, and had a gun to his head. I could only imagine what would have happened if I did not submit to the spirit of God that night. It is important to be obedient to the spirit of God and to do it when he places in your spirit to intercede on behalf of someone else. Your prayer just may stop the enemy's plan. For the effectual, fervent prayer of a righteous man availeth much (James 5:16). I am a living witness to the power of prayer and what your prayer can do. I could not operate in the ministry and the office God has called me to, without the foundation of prayer. I can remember times when I would pray all night, not seeing anything change in the natural but believing and knowing change was taking place in the spiritual realm and would soon manifest in the natural. After years of much prayer and fasting, my son is out of prison, after serving six years when, if taken to trial, he could have served fifteen to twenty-five years. I know that trusting and believing God changed his life. This came through thirteen years of just trusting God, walking by faith and not by sight.

Trust in the Lord with all thine heart and lean not unto thine own understanding. (Proverbs 3:5)

My Personal Experience with Prayer

If my people, which are called by my name, shall
humble themselves and pray, and seek my face.
—2 Chronicles 7:14, KJV

Communion with God... Prayer has become the most essential and important tool in my walk with God. Most importantly, I could not operate in the ministry and the office that God has called me to without the foundation of prayer. It is in my personal time in prayer that I draw closer to God, hear his voice, become more intimate with him, and experience his divine presence. As I draw closer to him, he draws closer to me (James 4:8). I'm in love with prayer; therefore, I am in love with my God, Jesus Christ, my Lord and Savior. Prayer became an essential element in my spiritual growth. Coupled together with the Word of God, it has become a powerful tool used against the forces of evil. The Word of God says that "when the enemy comes in like a flood the spirit of the Lord shall lift up a standard against him meaning Satan and his cohorts. For the weapons of our warfare are not carnal but mighty through God to the pulling down of strong holds" (2 Cor. 10:4). The spirit of the Lord is the Word, because he is the Word. In the beginning was the Word, and the Word was with God, and the Word was God. (John 1:1, NIV). Prayer and the Word are your weapons, because you need spiritual weapons to deal with Satan's weapons. There are many types of prayer. Jesus in Matthew 6:9–13 taught the disciples to pray. This prayer encompassed many areas including worshipping, reverencing and adoration toward God, concern for the Kingdom of God, his will being done, our needs being met, forgiveness, as well as deliverance. First John 1:9 gives us a prayer of confession; 1 Timothy 2:1–3 gives us a prayer of supplication; James 5:15, a prayer of faith; and Philippians 4:6, a prayer of thanksgiving.

Prayer is a powerful tool. Through prayer, we are able to build up our spirit man. This is why it is important to be filled with the spirit of God through the baptism of the Holy Spirit, which is the third person in the Trinity. It is the spirit that makes intercession for us when we don't know what to pray (Romans 8:26). When we go before God in prayer, we must be in right standing with God in order for him to hear and answer our prayer (John 9:31, Proverbs 1:28–30, Isaiah 1:15). God does not hear the prayer of a sinner except it be a prayer of repentance (John 9:31).

There were several occasions when God instructed Jeremiah not to intercede on behalf of Israel because of their broken covenant with God (Jeremiah 11:14). They continued to put other things before God, rebel against him, and go their own pernicious ways (Jeremiah 11:8–13). So we see here that if we continue in rebellion against God and his will, he will not answer our prayers. But if we, with our whole hearts, come to God, confess our sins, and have the intention of turning from our wicked ways, he is faithful and just to forgive our sins and cleanse us from all unrighteousness (1 John 1:9). So we must obey God and live according to his Word. The eyes of the Lord are upon the righteous, and his ears are open unto their cry (Psalms 34:15). If our hearts are full of iniquity, the Lord will not hear our prayers (Psalms 66:18). It is the effectual, fervent prayer of the righteous man that availed much (James 5:16). Sin in our hearts and in our lives hinders our prayers. We then must ask God for forgiveness and seek him for deliverance from anything that has a stronghold on our life and that is hindering our prayers.

One of the Hebrew words for *prayer* is *challah*, which means to be weak, to be sick, to be afflicted, to be wounded, to entreat, and to supplicate. This can be considered a travailing prayer. What is travailing prayer? Travailing prayer is when you pray from your belly out of your soul, in intensity as if you are in pain. Tears, bearing of a burden, and a groaning from within may be evident in travailing prayer. It is as if you are trying to bring something from within out. A travailing prayer is toiling prayer. This type of prayer causes you to cry out of your spirit. A perfect example of this type of prayer would be a mother who is about to give birth to a baby. She begins to experience contractions, and with the contractions, she endures pain. At this point, in order for the baby to be born, she has to push the baby through the birth canal, and along with her pushing, she is travailing (enduring pain) in the process.

Another word for *prayer* is the Greek word *deesis*, which means a petition, request, or supplication. When we make a petition, it is making a request for a desired need for the one who is praying or on behalf of another. In other words, we are humbly asking God to hear us and answer us, and then we wait, expecting to receive an answer from him. Sometimes we have to make our request known to God more than once. I don't think doing this is an indication that we don't believe God, but I think it is the total opposite, that we do believe God and as we are continuously making our request known to him, our faith and confidence in him is being built up. The Word of God tells us to pray without ceasing. Ask, and it shall be given you, seek and ye shall find, knock and it shall be opened unto you (1 Thessalonians 5:17, Luke 11:9). When you ask for something, you expect something back in return, whether it is a response to a question or receipt of something you ask for. When we seek something, we search for it in intensity, not letting up or giving in until we find what we are looking for. And when we knock, for example, on a door, we are knocking expecting someone to answer that door. If no one answers when we knock the first time, we continue to knock until someone answers. Still if there is no answer, we may decide to return at a later time or, to be more precise, to come back at a set time. It is the same thing with God. We have to be so set on expecting an answer or God to show up in our situation that we will search him out until we receive from the Lord. One thing we have to make sure of is that we are praying the will of God. The only way to know that we are praying the will of God is to know his word. So

God commands us to study to show ourselves approved unto God a workman who needeth not to be ashamed but rightly dividing the word of Truth (2 Timothy 2:15). If we pray what God's word says, we are guaranteed a return. His word is his promise to us, and his word will not return back void, but it will accomplish whatever it is sent out to do (Isaiah 55:11). When we send God's word out, it will prosper where it is sent. God's word is power, and when we use God's word, we have power with God. Death and life is right in front of us, in our mouth (Proverbs 18:21). So we must preserve our mouth and the words that come out of our mouth to be fruitful unto good.

I had to learn that lesson the hard way and can still take lessons on what to say, when to say it, and what not to say or just keep my mouth shut. The Word of God tells us the tongue is an unruly evil full of poison and that no man can tame it (James 3:8). This is why we need the Holy Spirit to help us, but it will also take some work on our part, self-control. Just like we learned habits through daily practice, we too must practice controlling our tongue. The Word of God tells us to study to be quiet (1 Thessalonians 4:11). In other words, when Paul wrote this letter to the Thessalonians, he was telling them to live a life that pleases God, a quiet, peaceful life, minding your own business. We are not to be busybodies in other people's matters (1 Timothy 5:13). Sometimes, the Lord will allow situations to arise that we will think it is an attack from the enemy when, in all reality, it is the Lord trying to teach us to keep our mouths shut and stop talking so much. If we cleanse our thoughts, our conversation will begin to be more edifying and fruitful. We will begin to build up others and not tear them down. Most of us need a heart transplant, because out of the heart, the mouth speaks.

God Forgave Me,
Why Couldn't I Forgive Me

If we confess our sins, he is faithful and just to forgive
[our] sins, and cleanse us from all unrighteousness.

—1 John1:9, KJV

It was April 1998 when I gave my life to the Lord for real. I remember the message my former pastor, the late Apostle William Brown, preached that Sunday morning, "Your Secret Is Out." It was like the Lord himself was talking directly to me. Yes, that day, my secret was out. God knew everything that I ever tried to hide. He also knew the sincerity of my heart that day. I was the first one down the aisle to the altar because that day was the day of salvation for me. I was brokenhearted, rejected, and most of all, tired of living outside the will of God. I did a little bit of everything in my life, but that day was the end of that life and the beginning of a new life for me. Even when I was living and doing what I wanted to do, I always cried out to God for help and read the twenty-seventh psalm. When I finally got to the front of the church, Apostle Brown said four words to me, "You love the Lord." And that I did, but there was always a battle going on, and I believe most of you can identify. That day, my life changed; I accepted Christ as my Lord and Savior (once again), was filled with his spirit, and began to fight to get my life back. You see, I was so confused and broken I didn't know if I was able to make it to another day, but that day was a new beginning for me.

From My Mother's Womb

*Before I formed thee in the belly I knew thee; and before
thou camest forth out of the womb I sanctified thee,
and ordained thee a prophet unto the nations.*
—Jeremiah 1:5, KJV

My mother told me of a time when she was getting on the bus with me (I was just a baby wrapped in a blanket), and she told me that a woman said to her, "This is a special baby." I always wonder why, growing up, I didn't feel special or felt I wasn't treated special but always felt rejected.

Sometimes I thought that if I do certain things, I would get the love and attention I always wanted, but then it was soon forgotten. So I escaped into another world, a world that no one else knew anything about, because it was my place of escape. This has always been something I battled with on a daily basis, should I live or should I die. I finally realized later on in life it was not for me to determine. I always had to do things to make an impression on someone else just to be accepted. This could be something very difficult to capture and keep a hold to, if you are always discouraged, never encouraged, and told you will never be anything. So those dreams were just an entourage of thought that kind of faded away. But when I look back, I am grateful because I didn't end up being something or someone that I didn't want to be.

My Beginning Is My End

I am the Alpha and the Omega, the First and
the Last, the Beginning and the End.
—Revelation 22:13, NIV

The beginning of new things for me is a way of allowing God to complete my end. Writing a book or a volume of books has always been a part of me. I had a professor who tried to encourage me to major in English literature, but I always thought what would I do with that. Where would it take me? Sometimes we don't see past our own selves and realize that our lives are not even our own and that God is the one that orders our steps if we allow him to. When you are born with purpose and called from your mother's womb, no matter what you do or how you try to do it, if God is not in it, it will not prosper. I didn't think this would be a part of my purpose and call. I didn't imagine that this could be a part of completing my end and leaving a legacy behind. One thing I do know for sure now is that this is one of my assignments. This book is all for the glory of God. My prayer is that this book will minister or even change the lives of others. Getting started was a task because my life entailed so much drama. As a child, I always felt like the black sheep, different and couldn't meet anyone's expectations. This was the way I felt not just as a child but as a young adult as well. Some things never change unless you purpose in your heart that some things must change to get better results. Change had to take place in order for me to be the person I was created to be, who God created me to be.

As an adult, people have always been a part of my dilemma. I guess that's why my prayer has been "Lord, deliver me from people." It wasn't just the person, but I played a role as well. I had to be delivered from always wondering what people thought about me and what they said about me and just wanting to be accepted. Being this way always put me in a position of hiding who I really was and what I was really feeling. Now I look at those same words and realize that in ministry or just life itself, you have to deal with people and you can't escape from them. People are the ones that make ministry. So I guess this made me look at myself and say, "What is it in me that I must change?" People are not always the problem, and we are not always the victim. I have to look at myself and say, "Am I allowing my past to control my present and eventually dictate my future, or am I showing love toward others the way the Bible say I should?" So I guess this has drastically changed my prayer to "God, I want to give birth to the fruit of the spirit, and teach me how to love right." I'm in a process, and it is still not complete. I must genuinely realize that whatever I was called to do is not about me; it's about what God has predestined me to be and completing the work he gives me. If God spoke a word for you to complete an assignment, you have to complete that assignment before you can move on to the next assignment. We can't move forward in the things of God if we can't follow his instructions. In other words, we have to walk in obedience. I believe my problem has always been putting too much focus on what the end would be instead of staying in my beginning. It's okay to dream, but what you do with the dream is the question. We have to take the dream out of our heads and grasp it with our hands, meaning to grab hold of it, and make it a reality.

The word of God tells us that being confident of this very thing, that he which hath begun a good work in you will perform *it* until the day of Jesus Christ (Philippians 1:6). Only God knows our end. It is our confidence in Christ that we develop according to his will for our lives and do not go in our own way. Sometimes, we want things to happen in our timing, but there is a time and season that the things that God has promised us will manifest in our lives. There are conditions as well to receiving the blessings of the Lord. First, we have to know what the will of God is for our lives, and the only way that we will know this is through his word and prayer. So we need to ask ourselves, Are we doing the things that God requires us to do? Are we in the will of God? Do our lives line up with his will for our lives? God sometimes gives us a glimpse of what's to come, but just enough to encourage us to press forward. When these little peeks into our future come, especially when we are experiencing difficult times in our lives, they encourage us to remind us that God will fulfill his promises in our lives, and it builds up our faith; it fortifies us. For me, these little glimpses keep me motivated, focused, and on track when I get sidetracked.

As a child, I always felt I had to get all As in school; if not, my self-image went down a notch. Wanting to get all As caused me to study harder so that I could reach that goal, but the results were not always all As but that I did my best and worked hard. The same level of motivation that I put into getting As in school is the same motivation I have to put into what God assigns me to do. I was always teased at school, always an emotional wreck, and this had an impact on my self-esteem, how I saw myself. My older sisters said that, as a child, I was a spoiled brat, whatever that means. Since my mother had to work all the time, I was oftentimes watched by my sister. As I got older, in seventh grade, I started experimenting with drugs. So I would go to school high on marijuana. It seemed to be the fun and the "in" thing to do, but as time passed, it became a serious problem. I began experimenting and using other drugs. I wanted to be loved and found myself in and out of abusive relationships. Now when I say *abuse*, I don't just mean physical abuse but psychological and emotional abuse. This kind of abuse can be just as bad as physical abuse and leave you emotionally scarred, and these are usually scars that are not visibly seen, because you are scarred inside. So my drugs became another relationship for me just to try to ease the pain and remove the depression. This is when all the emotional drama began in my life. At age fourteen, I made my first suicide attempt, and I saw death, but God put life back in me, and it was nothing but the hand of God on my life.

I don't know why my thoughts keep drifting back to my childhood. God is about to deliver and heal the person reading this from their past. I believe that a lot of innate behaviors are portrayed in our adult lives. I was allowed to suck a bottle until I was six years old, and as a little girl, I was a guardian angel for my dad by escorting him home when he was intoxicated. It had to be nothing but the grace of God that guided us home. I didn't find out my dad was not my biological dad until I was nineteen years old. Even though I don't remember the exact day, I still remember the pain and betrayal I felt on that day. I wanted so badly for my stepfather to be my biological father because he was the only father I knew since I was a baby. Other family members knew except me. I always said I looked like my dad, and no one ever told me differently. I was living a lie, but he loved me and took me as his own, and I could remember the tears he cried when I found out he was not my biological dad. I did eventually meet my biological father, but we never developed a lasting relationship, but it's okay today. I tried to contact him after we lost contact, but to no avail. At least I had the opportunity to meet him and speak to him on several occasions.

Many times I used to feel like my life was nothing but a lie, a big mistake. Maybe that is the reason why I felt like I had to always prove myself. When I failed to meet the expectations of others, I resorted to drugs and many suicide attempts and looked for love in all the wrong places. My life was full of emotional breakdowns, suicide attempts, disappointments, and rejection.

I remember the first time I tried to overdose on pills. I took some of every kind of drugs that were available in the medicine cabinet, from prednisone to high blood pressure medications. It didn't matter to me what I was taking and how much I took; I just didn't want to hurt anymore. I wanted it to just go away. I wanted to die. Since pain had become a daily part of my life, I allowed not wanting to feel the pain of rejection by giving up my virginity and ended up hurt in the end anyway. I accepted sex as love, compromise as acceptance, and losing myself in a fantasy world as happiness. My self-esteem had diminished. I didn't know myself, couldn't find myself, and felt like at times that I didn't even exist. I was numb to who I was.

I remember my mother sent me away to live with my sister because she couldn't deal with me anymore. There was that feeling of rejection again and not feeling wanted, not even by my own mother. Yes, I was considered the black sheep in the family, and I lived in a black abyss. I felt that way most of the time, but later on in life, I came to realize I am just different. Little did my mother know that handing me over to my sister was not going to fix me and things would get worse. I was soon on my way back to New York because, I guess, my sister realized she couldn't fix me either. So you see, I was on an emotional roller coaster most of my life until Christ called me and I said yes.

I always wondered why life had to be full of changes. Now I realize that change is part of growth. Growth is essential in our development and helps us in seeing life from different perspectives. When you think about it, life would be nothing in itself if change didn't take place. Everything and everyone, except God, has to go through the process of change. Without change, there would be no purpose in life. We need purpose to grow. For example, even a butterfly has purpose. From the time the female monarch lays an egg on a leaf, purpose comes into existence. The ultimate purpose is to reach full maturity so that the butterfly life cycle will begin all over again. We too have purpose, and this purpose is in reaching our fullest potential in what God created us to become.

How do you deal with your process of change? How do you respond to the process of change? What is the process of change like? We know everyone's experience is different in so many dimensions. So first, I will deal with the natural perspective of the process of change and then the spiritual perspective of the process of change. We, as recipients of change, have to make the decision to want to change, so that takes some initiative on our part. Naturally, we are comfortable with the way we do things on a routine basis, even the way we have been programmed to think a particular way. Change can be traumatic to many and, at times, may have a psychological effect on many. For example, a person has lived with a caretaker for many years, and suddenly the caretaker dies, so that person has to adjust to the fact that they will never see that person again and that the things that the caretaker did for them, they have to begin to do for themselves, or someone else has to do them. The biggest adjustment the person has to make is living without that person.

Now from a spiritual perspective, change is crucial and constant if we want to grow in the things of God. We have to change our way of thinking. Our minds have to be renewed daily (Romans 12:2). When our lives are transformed, we begin to experience a more intimate relationship with God. God's will becomes our will. We seek to be more like him by praying, studying his Word, and being not just a hearer of the Word but a doer as well (James 1:22). The Hebrew word for *process* is *rabah*, which means to increase. So when we go through the process, we can focus not on how painful it may be but on what it will produce in and through us in the end. We have to keep in mind that all things are working together for our good (Romans 8:28) and he that has begun a good work in you will perform it (Philippians 1:6). From a spiritual perspective, it is a time of preparation that the Lord takes you through to get you to the place he wants you to be in. This process can consist of trials great and small, disappointments, doubts, rejection, pain, loss, as well as gains and victories. Most of the time, the process is God's way of purifying us, and this in itself can be painful because we have to break past things that we are familiar with and that have become habitual. These things can cause us to become comfortable, and we become complacent in moving forward in God. When we go through the process, we grow spiritually and mature. Eventually, this process allows us to deal with areas in our lives that have caused us to suffer unnecessarily. In other words, we most likely will experience deliverance from things we didn't see as a problem, so we have to repeat that process. We should develop character and integrity, which, above all, speaks for the fruit of the spirit that has been developed in our lives. For me, having the fruit of the spirit is priority, because I believe that when you have properly developed them, everything else follows.

For me, consistency in praying, fasting, and studying his word; obedience to the spirit of God; and developing and cultivating the right relationships have to be something I have to master if I want to fulfill purpose in my life. I can't start something and not finish it, because if I do, I go on to something else, and what I first started will eventually not be a priority. Instead of it being a short-term goal, it ends up becoming a long-term goal or a goal that never reaches completion. I don't want to be a jack-of-all-trades and a master of none. I have to stay focused. I can't allow things to distract me or else my focus is broken. I have had many disappointments along the way, but one thing I have concluded is, even when I want to give up, feel like giving up, or say "What's the use?" I keep moving forward. I can say that God has favored me and graced me in this season in my life. If it wasn't for him, I could not do or be anything. When you have a dream and passion for something, it can be very discouraging when you pursue your dream and things don't work out the way you planned it to. So I come to realize that God has another plan, a better plan, and a better way. To be able to pursue my dreams, my passion for God has to supersede my passion for my passion. In other words, if I have that same passion for God or even greater, I can't fail.

There are things that I have to get in order in my life, just believing God and not stopping in trusting him. I have to revisit some places in my mind and emotions that I thought I would never have to revisit again. But this is part of the process for me. It is a process I cannot escape because it is what will make me into the person God created me to be. Yes, we all have to go through the process. Deliverance is a process. Healing is a process. Sanctification is a process. Life itself is a process. To live, we have to go through constant changes and transitions. If we want to know how to love after all we know is anger and bitterness, we have to go through a process called change. Now don't get me wrong; I am not saying this process will happen instantaneously. Believe me, I know; I had to battle anger and unforgiveness most of my life. These two things led to many places in my life I would not have had to go if I had made the right choices: the choice to forgive and the choice to love unconditionally. It is going to take the power of God once you are delivered, to maintain your deliverance. It is going to take much diligence as well as discipline.

You will have to be diligent in your prayer life; reading the Word of God and fasting should also be a part of your maintenance process. The Word of God transforms us into the image and likeness of his son, Jesus Christ, and his Word washes us. When we partake of his Word, because he is the Living Word, we are renewed daily. You see, the spirit is willing, but the flesh is weak (Matthew 26:41). There is nothing good about our flesh except that it covers our body for protection against disease. The body's skin or flesh shields the body from parasites, bacteria, or viruses that cause disease. The skin also alerts the immune system of the presence of harmful bacteria. If this protective barrier is broken, we are prone to being attacked by things that can harm our bodies. Just like how the flesh or skin is a physical barrier to protect our bodies, the Holy Spirit is a spiritual barrier to protect our soul. In order for this barrier to not be broken, we have to keep it healthy by nourishing it with the Word of God and prayer. Praying in the spirit helps us build up or edify our spirit. The Word of God tells us that "he that speaketh with an unknown tongue edifieth himself" (1 Corinthians 14:4). If we allow our spirit (barrier) to be broken or tainted, we risk forfeiting our relationship with God.

If I were to choose someone from the Bible that I would want to be like, I would choose Anna. She is only mentioned once in the Bible and in a small portion of scripture, yet she has a powerful testimony. In that small portion of scripture, I can concur that Anna is described to be a woman who knew God. Why? Because she stayed in the presence of God (Luke 2:37). She was so hungry for God; she never departed from the temple but served God day and night with prayer and fasting. What power she had with God. I thought about what kind of woman Anna must have been. I concluded she was a woman of purpose, had the mind of the spirit, and was a true woman of God devoted to his will and a woman of spiritual wisdom and profound knowledge of scriptures. She had high standards when it came to the things of God, had great love for God and his people, and was a woman of strength, a woman of humility and submission. And she knew how to wait on God and depend on him to sustain her.

I have come to the realization that bad choices or decisions can hinder our process. When we make decisions based particularly on our emotions, that decision becomes an at-that-moment decision. We must realize that the feeling will pass, but we become so caught up in the moment we become trapped by living out that moment, and for some of us, it can become a lifetime commitment based on that decision. At that time, our process becomes a hindrance instead of a blessing because we allowed our emotions and not the spirit to be in charge.

Living out of your emotions can be detrimental to your psychological, mental, physical, and spiritual growth. Our emotions coincide with spontaneous rational decision-making. What we have to realize at the time of emotional arousal is that our mental state has been disturbed and that there is a lack in the ability to make conscious decisions. Our feelings become so aroused that most often our thought processes have been dismissed for that moment. Some of us are emotionalist because our conduct, behaviors, thoughts, and relationship with Christ are governed by our emotions, leaving no room for reasoning or making sound decisions. These people are usually the ones who live in pure regret, self-pity, or if-only-I-had mode most of their lives.

Have you ever found yourself wanting to appease others for the sake of being accepted? Well, I have. Because of so much rejection in my past, I always felt a need to be accepted. Even now I have to be very careful not to backslide into that same abyss. Yes, I call it an abyss, a deep black hole, because it becomes a place of bondage, a place where you find yourself always wanting to validate yourself, but you can't because this place is dark and void. You can't see where there is no light. The only way to escape this place of imprisonment is to receive the light, which is Jesus Christ, and know who *he is* in your life.

You see, as a child growing up, I lived in a world where I was afraid to fail, because I knew the pain of that failure and what mental state I would end up in. As you can recall, my entire life was linked to depression until it became my favorite enemy. I became so used to being depressed I began to believe that was the way I was supposed to feel. I didn't know what it was to be happy. When you begin to believe you're supposed to feel or be a certain way, that is what you become. I would always hear the words "We love you" or "Do you know what this is doing to the people that love you?" Oh, I forgot to mention every time I would go into depression, I would contemplate taking my life; everyone seemed to not notice or pay attention to what I needed. But what I realized is that they couldn't give me what I needed and that I would only find fulfillment and deliverance in Christ.

I can remember to this day the first time the enemy was out to snatch my life. It was on a day I was coming home from school. My school was just two blocks away from where I lived. I usually would walk with some of my classmates who went in the same direction I had to go until we arrived at the main avenue and departed. My mother was usually at work, and at that time, the daughter of my mother's deceased sister lived with us. On this particular day after walking home, I arrived at my building and waited for the elevator, and when I got on the elevator, a tall dark-skinned man with a beige trench coat and a thick black mustache came in behind me. With nowhere to run, I got a feeling that I was in danger. I pressed the floor I was to get off at, which was the top floor. Then something inside me told me to get off the elevator. So I pressed another floor and got off and began to run up the stairs, scared and petrified. When I arrived at the sixth floor, so did the elevator with the man on it. He looked through the glass window of the elevator door. At that time, my cousin happened to be in the hallway talking to her friend, who was our next-door neighbor. He never got off the elevator but went back down. Even as I tell about this particular event in my life, I can remember his face so vividly. You can only imagine the fear and terror I felt on that day. Today, I know that man's intention was to take me to the roof, rape me, and kill me. The devil had planned that day to take my life, but God intervened. The devil might have had a hit on your life from a young age because he knew that you were created for a purpose and would do damage to his kingdom.

My life was never a bed of roses but a life of emotional, mental, sexual, and verbal abuse. And the funny thing about it is that a lot of the abuse came from those who said they loved me. I was even sexually violated by our next-door neighbor's son. My mother would send me to the next-door neighbor's house to get the newspaper, and the neighbor's son would answer the door and take me to his room.

When I finally told someone, who was my cousin, the neighbor said I was lying. Eventually, something was done. Later on in life, I found out that he was in prison and he died from AIDS. But for those who are reading this book and are broken, I'm here to tell you that God can fix you and there is deliverance. I know because I am a living testimony. I visited so many psychiatric facilities in my lifetime that they became my second home. Every time I went to one, God always had someone there to minister to me. It got to the point that I would find myself encouraging others who were emotionally and mentally broken. So you see, I had to go through the things I went through so that the ministry God has placed in me can be manifested and used for his glory. I'm not saying that everything in my life has been perfected, but I am not the same person I was, and today I know who I am. I'm not saying I am on a street called Easy, because every day I am in a spiritual battle. But in this battle, Christ fights for me. This is a different fight. This is a fight I cannot and will not lose. There is a determination in me that causes me to fight the good fight of faith. I can't go back. There is nothing for me to go back to but death. I remember some years ago, my former pastor, Apostle William Brown, told me that if I go back, the devil will kill me. The trials are even greater, but God gives me the strength to endure, and I know he will not put too much on me that I cannot bear.

Writing this book is not an easy task, but it has to be written. It is a mandate from the Lord that, for me, is way overdue. This book will not only bring me to full deliverance and recovery, but deliverance, healing, and recovery will also take place for those that read this book.

I remember as plain as day on October 26, 2008, the spirit of the Lord visited me in the early part of the day when I fell into a deep sleep. It was then that God gave me my instructions in writing this book, and thereafter, it has been confirmation after confirmation. This is only the beginning of a pathway through the process of deliverance. My desire is that I want to see others delivered and set free from the enemy's grip.

Adonai (Lord, Master)

The Lord is my light and my salvation,
whom shall I fear? The Lord is the strength of my life;
of whom shall I be afraid?

—Psalms 27:1 KJV

Psalm 27 has been my favorite psalm throughout the course of my life: when I was not a born-again Christian and when I became a born-again Christian, when I didn't know God and when I knew him. I believe this psalm brought me through many tough times in my life. It reminded me that God is my Lord and because of him, I can live and not die.

I started writing the book and then stopped. I kept starting, but then I would stop again. I didn't want to go through the pain of reliving my past once again. It was painful, but I kept telling myself I must finish my assignment. I asked the Lord to help me, to strengthen me, to give me what I need, and to give him what he wants. The bottom line is that it all boils down to obedience. Two years later, I visited a church for the first time. I didn't know anyone, and I started feeling a little bit uncomfortable. I began to talk to God and ask him, "Lord, if this is you moving in this place and you led me here by your spirit, I need you to show yourself to me once again and send a word, Lord. I was at a point in my life where I needed to see the manifestation of the Lord in my life. I waited, but nothing. So I decided that I was going to leave. Soon after that thought, the man of God, Bishop W.

E. Holmes, walked over to me and began to minister to me. This is the word of the Lord that he spoke over my life:

> Woman of God, there are major things that are about to happen in your life. You're in a shift. You know the change has come. You know there are mental things you have locked in the spirit realm. There are major things you are to partake, even in this hour that the devil has been trying to keep from you. Actually, the thing that God has shifted you into was to help you develop in the place where God wants you to go into. There is a place. There is a book inside of you, and that book has got to be written, but you have been putting it down. *There is the confirmation again* [emphasis mine]. Seems like the more you put it down, the more you keep going back to it. You put it down and go back. But I hear the Word of the Lord say there is an author, and you're going to author that book. Come 2012, in the beginning of 2012, you will see in the right place, because there are some things you have to do in the next few months. By the beginning of 2012, that book should be published, and it shall be up in the front, and there shall be some new things that shall come out. The Word of the Lord has been sitting very strong inside of you, because God has been saying, because I have been sitting resident for the next season you're going to walk into, and it has been those who stood by you and thought you were off. And you kept saying, 'Lord, I believe you. I believe what you told me because you did not lie,' and because you kept trusting God, God kept escalating and pulling you into new dimensions of his grace and truth. This is the season that you're in, and the prophetic oil that's

inside of you is about to burst forth, and God's going to give clarity to it so you will never have to settle for a place where there will be no more clarity. Your ears will be open; your eyes will be open. Even your throat for the Word of the Lord to speak into will become open, an open sepulchre for you to hear what God is saying. This is going to be a new day for you, woman, a new day where nothing shall be the same, and fruit shall come forth out of you, saith the spirit of grace. And even those that are around you, your family members—they shall be settled. Settlement, settlement, settlement...and all shall be well, saith the spirit of grace.

You see, this book was supposed to be completed and published in 2012. Disobedience is a sin. When God places a mandate on our lives to do something, there is a purpose he has in us to do exactly what he calls us to do. This went on for four to five years, and for four to five years, I have hindered the blessings of the Lord from flowing in my life in its fullness. I suffered from many things I didn't have had to if I had not walked in disobedience. At times, we may feel we are doing everything that God requires us to do, like fasting, praying, reading and studying the Word, but sometimes he asks us to do those things to test our faith and to see if we will just listen and follow.

It is important to be obedient to the spirit of God. When we are obedient, we are in the will of God. We will eat the good of the land and enjoy its many benefits.

If you are willing and obedient you will eat the good of the land, but if you refuse and rebel, you will be eaten by the sword, for the mouth of ADONAI has spoken. (Isaiah 1:19, CJB)

With obedience comes a lot of responsibilities. For example, we have to develop an appetite for the things of God. In other words, if we read the Word of God daily and spend time with him in prayer, we develop a habit that benefits our spiritual growth. If we are obedient to what God requires of us, he can trust us with more. Many of us want the blessings of the Lord to overtake us but don't do what God's Word says to do. We can't live in any way we want to and then expect the fullness of God's glory in our lives. There are conditions to receiving God's blessings; our lives have to line up with his Word. Having an intimate relationship with God is key. By intimacy, I mean spending quality time with him in prayer. Communication is key in any relationship. Even though God knows everything about us, he still wants to talk with us. When we communicate with someone, we come to know them better. We discover their likes and dislikes. We come to like being with them, and as the relationship grows, we begin to feel a sense of trust and closeness with them. This is also true when we spend time with God. He begins to reveal more of himself to us as we make ourselves more available to him.

I'm not saying that because I have not completed this book at a certain time, God has not blessed me. I am blessed and continue to receive the blessings of the Lord daily. He supplies all my needs. He has been with me through every trial I had to endure. He has healed me of every sickness, and my life itself is a blessing. When I can share with others what God has done for me and brought me through, my life is a blessing itself, because my life can be used to encourage and bless someone else. I have come to realize that my life didn't happen by chance and that Satan tried to take my life from a young age not because he had nothing better to do but because he saw that God had handpicked me for such a time as this and that I would be part of a remnant that would do damage to his kingdom. I have an assignment from God on my life, and the devil doesn't like it. Every time he tries to take me out, I come back stronger and ready for the next battle. I am more than a conqueror through Christ Jesus who strengthens me. And no weapon formed against me can prosper, and every tongue that rises against me the Christ in me will condemn. What I want to point out is that when we are disobedient, we hinder the blessings of the Lord from flowing in our lives. God wants to have a trust relationship with us. Just as we want others to trust us, God expects the same response from us. He wants us to obey his Word and live life to the fullest according to his Word. We are in this world, but we are not of this world. So to the world we are to look and act differently.

Anger

Be angry without sinning. Don't go to bed angry.
Don't give the devil any opportunity to work.
—Ephesians 4:26,27 GWT

Living with anger on a daily basis is a fight in itself. It seems like the anger has overtaken you to a point of no return. No matter how hard you pray for deliverance each day, it seems like it will never come. You put all your efforts into not becoming angry, but soon something that reminds you of your past or a current situation you have been struggling with causes you to be tempted to go back to that place again. You begin to look at people around you: family, friends, and even strangers. Everyone appears to be so perfect, but when they close the door shut, their own personal battle begins. I know because I was one of those people. Sometimes, we are so used to lining up to what others expect of us that putting on a mask becomes second nature. We smile when we're hurting, we laugh when we really want to cry, we bend the truth just a little bit so we will appear as if we got it all together, and above all, we are perpetrating a fraud.

First, I need to explain what anger is and what it is not. Anger is a manifestation of a spirit. There are several spirits that anger is manifested from—one being carnality, which comes from the Greek word *sarkikos*, which connotes "rotten flesh" in English. By nature, it is in no way spiritual because its only assignment is to satisfy the appetite of the soul. Carnality invites in lust of the flesh, eyes and the pride of life (1 John 2:16), but there is another manifestation of anger I want to expound on, and that is a spirit that the majority of the body of Christ has battled—the spirit of rejection. We all, at one time or another, have been confronted by situations in which we felt rejected. As a child, rejection became a part of growing up for me. A lot of us, like myself, were not always accepted by others or never seemed to fit in. When attacked by the spirit of rejection, many areas of our lives are attacked: our self-worth, having difficulty trusting, experiencing an overwhelming, intensive feeling of emotional pain, insecurity taking root, having a low self-esteem, as well as anger.

Anger can be so damaging to our well-being that we end up hurting not only ourselves but also our relationships with other people in our lives. We say things in the heat of anger that we later regret, realizing at that point that we can never take those words back. Anger can cause us to build a wall between us and others, and we only invite people behind that wall, only to find out in the end that they are battling the same things we are battling. I can talk about this because this was once me, but I experienced many manifestations of the spirit of rejection: depression, bitterness, hopelessness, thoughts about suicide, giving my body for sex thinking I will receive love, emotional instability, lack of confidence in myself, and insecurity. Even today I may be confronted with some of these things, but it is how I respond to it that determines the outcome in the end. I can't allow the enemy access in these areas if I am to remain free. When I'm confronted with doubt, I have to release faith; when I'm confronted with hopelessness, I have to release hope; and when I don't want to forgive, I have to forgive (1 Corinthians 13:13, Matthew 6:12). I have to make these relevant virtues in my life in order to stay free. You see, when the enemy has tried to take your mind and keep you locked up in a mental prison, you have no choice but to fight to keep and maintain your sanity. I don't want to live in bondage, but I want to live a life of freedom and total dependency on Christ and his spirit to do a complete work in me.

Let this mind be in *me* that was also in Christ Jesus (Philippians 2:5). How many times have I said this scripture? I believe I have lost count. The mind is so powerful. You can think yourself into a situation and wonder how you got there. Okay, I guess I will speak for myself. Right now I need God to do some things in me. Yes, I am writing this book with the prayer that someone will be delivered, but you know what, this also is part of my deliverance. What is deliverance, and how do we stay delivered? Well, I don't have a definitive answer for you. Why? Because my deliverance, just like my sanctification, is a daily process. Again, the battle for me comes in maintaining my deliverance. I will seek the face of God through prayer and fasting, come to a place where there has been a release in my spirit, and get comfortable, only to realize I'm back to where I was before battling that same demon. Okay, some of you may not have experienced this, but I have to be transparent because I have some things that I need God to deliver me from. For example, when I am hurting, I justify my pain by talking about it, which leads to talking about those involved and those that hurt me, and the bottom line is, I have just stepped over into a prohibited zone, a place that I am familiar with that I have no place being, because I should have maintained my deliverance. I have to now go before God, again, repent, and ask him to help me overcome this thing that keeps pushing me back into bondage, because I allowed my emotions (flesh) to take precedence over my spirit. My desire is to stay free, but one thing I have come to realize is that freedom doesn't mean I'm not going to be in any constant warfare. The warfare is even greater. Prayer is essential, along with fasting and staying in the Word of God, if I want to stay free. I can't go back to doing the old things I used to do when I have stepped into the new. To stay free is a constant battle. I have to stay in close proximity with God. I can't break intimate fellowship with him. If I do, I'm in trouble. I have to constantly remind myself to stay focused and that some things are just a distraction to get me offtrack. We have to know when the enemy is trying to take us out. We have to be in constant watch for the attacks. The more we press toward the things of God, the more the devil presses on us. We have to keep our hearts with all diligence. Never let our guard down; always be properly dressed for battle. When we follow the pattern that the Lord has mapped out for us in his Word, we can rest in the Lord and experience the peace of God that passes all understanding.

I remember some years ago, my former pastor who has gone home to be with the Lord, Apostle William Brown, told me, "If you go back, the devil is going to kill you." The Lord revealed to me it's my mind the devil is after. If he has your mind, he has you.

I have had the devil tell me I was going to lose my mind, and there had been times that I literally felt like I was losing my mind. But there is something in me that I call the fight in me where I can't give in to the enemy's trap.

I know God to be a healer of the mind, because when others and I thought I would never be right, God made my mind right. You see, the psychiatric hospital and mental institutions were my second home away from home before I surrendered to Christ.

I remember I had a dream that I went back to a mental institution to help all these women escape and we had to move quickly because security (the devil) was coming after us to stop us. There were so many women I couldn't even count them. We ended up coming face-to-face with a wall (spiritual bondage) with nowhere else to turn. So I decided that I would climb the wall and go over, leading all the women over the wall (spiritual freedom).

You are probably wondering what that has to do with anything. I am a firm believer that when God has brought you out from a situation, it is so you can go back and help others out of the same situation. Who would be the best candidates for the assignment but the ones who have been through it themselves?

There is always a battle in the mind. Sometimes it is like the mind never rests, always thinking, always debating, always wondering, sometimes thinking about giving up, sometimes doubting. I have come to the true realization that there is always going to be this thing that constantly wars in the mind. But what would I do in a world I once knew? It was a world that caused me much pain and rejection without ever finding comfort. There is life you must choose. Defeat is not a part of that life. Once you find yourself, you won't recognize defeat because it has become uncommon ground to you. It's your soul that you want back, the soul that God intended for you to have. In Genesis 2:7, the Lord formed man from the dust of the ground and breathed into his nostrils the breath of *life*, and man became a *living soul*. It's a place where your spirit completely and totally dominates your whole entire being.

Being a very analytic person, at times overanalytic, my mind has always been a target for the enemy. It seems like it is a never-ending battle. Even right now as I penned these words, before the pen touched the page, I was in a mind battle. I pray and lay hands on myself. I apply the blood and ask God to help me because at times, I feel like I am losing my mind. When my mind is not stable, everything about me and in me is unstable. I experience all kinds of emotions and feelings. At times, they can be so evident, yet I can't explain them due to the overwhelming intensity of them. I want to talk to someone thinking they will understand, but at the same time, I have to be careful of wanting someone to feel sorry for me. I just have to be honest because I just want to stay free and see someone else receive their deliverance. It doesn't matter what others think, feel, or say about me when my life is on the line because my deliverance is about me. I am desperate for deliverance to be a daily part of my life as God purifies me. Yes, I want every part of me to be like Jesus, but then the mind tells me to stop trying. And then I believe that it is when I truly stop trying that God can and will do it in me. There has always been a part of me that wishes I can start my life all over again, go back into my mother's womb, and have a new birth experience. I would do things differently than what I've done. I would make different choices.

Yes, this book is about my battles and my deliverance—not just past deliverance, but my daily deliverance. Lord, deliver my soul in peace from the battle *that is within me* (Psalms 55:8). It's not about the call, it's not about the God-given gifts in you, and it's not about how well or how often you may pray. All that sounds good, but if the soul is not right, it's just a mask, a way of escaping the reality of the person you are and need to change.

I Refuse to Die

*The thief cometh not, but to steal, and to kill, and
to destroy: I am come that they might have life, and
that they might have it more abundantly.*
—John 10:10, KJV

There are two kinds of death: physical and spiritual. In my lifetime
thus far, I have experienced both, depending on how you define *to
die*. Physical death, for me, was dying to my will and being obedient
to the will of God. I felt the pain in the very core of my being. Up
until this point in my life, I can say that I have experienced physical
death on several occasions at different times. I don't think anyone
wants to die. The Bible views death as the time when the soul is separated from the body (James 2:26). Sometimes when we go through
a physical death (our flesh being crucified), we may also experience a
spiritual death. We feel like God is not with us, but the Word of God
says, "He will never leave us nor forsake us" (Deuteronomy 31:6).

When I died physically (submitting my flesh to the will of
God), I developed a new desire to live, a desire to live that emulated
once I was resuscitated. I will never know that person I once was, but
it would be a testimony of the person God delivered me from. This
too would give me the desire to live a life from a different perspective.

At times, it can be difficult not to reflect on the memories of
the old you, especially when that person was birthed from a breed
that had no direction, no potential investment in a life that can eventually change the lives of others one day. The life that I live now is
a life that I believe can breathe life into others and bring about a

radical change. I have that kind of faith to believe that everything I went through and experienced in my life was to help bring someone else out of their pit. This comes not from what someone has told me but from what I had to go through. A radical change happened in me, and I have been called to bring about a change in the lives of others. My life holds a key to open a door in someone else's life. That is my purpose. This change helped me genuinely realize I can't change others but the change in my life can effect and bring about change in the lives of others. Like others, my childhood had a lot of painful experiences that altered my life in many ways. It brought about a testimony in me, and the Word of God says, "We overcome by the words of our testimony" (Revelation 12:11). I have overcome sickness, low self-esteem, suicidal ideations, depression, and allowing what others say about me or how others feel about me to affect me. Like I said, I can't change people, but my change can bring about change in others.

Change can be difficult, especially if the state you allow yourself to stay in has been a part of your self-existence for so long. This can be eradicated, and I am a living testimony to that taking place. We have to begin our change process from within. It begins with the heart. Our spirit is nourished by our soul, and then the soul nourishes the heart. The heart is the first place of deposit. The Word of God tells us to keep our hearts with all diligence, for out of it are the issues of life (Proverbs 4:23).

I heard many times prophetically that we are in a year of double: double anointing, double blessing, everything good, double. Right now I feel like I am in a year of double trials, double pain, and double everything except what God promised me. I am being stripped again of everything. I ask the Lord, "Why?" and there is no response. What do you do when God is silent? You keep praying. You keep seeking. You keep fasting. You keep waiting. Soon your breakthrough is coming. One thing I do realize is that through my tears, the pain, and everything I'm going through and have been through, God is with me. How do I know this? Because I still have my sanity, and I am able to give God my worship. I still go to him in prayer. I still keep seeking him. To tell you the truth, God is really speaking volumes as we go through our trials. He believes that if I can go through whatever I am going through, he can trust me to continue to have faith in him. His faith and trust in me speaks those volumes. It is like he is saying, "You can handle it." God does not allow us to be tested or tempted above what we are able to handle (1 Corinthians 10:13). At times, God has to put so much pressure on us that all that will be revealed is his glory in our lives. Flesh has to die. The greater the anointing, the greater the pressure. Most of us don't like pressure. Well, who does? I know I don't, but I come to realize that if I have purpose, I will survive. There are some things in me that I can't take to the place that God is taking me. Whatever you have to go through, God anoints you to go through it. He gives you what you need to carry the weight of the trails, but he takes the burden of that weight.

> *Come unto me, all ye that labour and are heavy laden and I will give you rest. Take my yoke upon you, and learn of me; for I am meek and lowly in heart: and ye shall find rest unto your souls. For my yoke is easy and my burden light.* (Matthew 11:28–30)

Transition

*Have not I commanded thee? Be strong and of good
courage: be not afraid, neither be thou dismayed: for the
Lord thy God is with thee withersoever thou goest.*
—Joshua 1:9, KJV

This is where I am. I don't understand exactly how this process works, but I'm in it for the long haul. I faced many setbacks, trials, discouragements and even wanted to give up. Even as I am writing, I am facing some of these things. At times, I find myself in a black hole, trying to find my way out, but I can't. It's dark. No one is there to help, and that's okay. One thing we must remember is, people will not always fully understand where you are and why you are where you are, and you know what, you may have those that don't understand at all. Whatever we go through is not for others to have a testimony but to give us a testimony to help others get through what they are going through.

During this transition, I am finding myself and realizing that people are just people. And when in transition, some people are not a part of that transition. Everyone can't go where God is taking you, and some people are actually a hindrance to your purpose if you allow them to be. They can be sent to try to sabotage your destiny. I know my struggles, I know what I am lacking, I know what I need to be doing, but the reality of it is, I just don't feel like doing it at times. Because of the way I have felt, it has caused me to miss God many times in the past. I'm tired physically, mentally, and emotionally. I figured it out though. I set high standards for myself, but when they don't come through, I'm right back to where I started. Frustration has been one of those places lately. I'm not trying to justify my situation, but the only way I will conquer this thing is to get to the root of it. There has been bitterness and unforgiveness, and a lot of it is from childhood hurts, those wounds that I have camouflaged with a smile or just by simply saying "I'm fine" when I'm not. If you are or have been in this place, only God can fix you. At times, I feel like how I used to feel after I would have a seizure. I have it and don't remember anything after that. My prayers during those times have been "Help me, God." I know that one day, I will look back and see the blessings that came out of everything I had to endure.

Childhood Scars

You have allowed me to suffer much hardship, but you will restore
me to life again and lift me up from the depths of the earth.
—Psalms 71:20, NLT

As a child, I can remember being beaten by my mother and the look
on her face as she was beating me. There was so much anger and bitterness I saw in her eyes that I began to believe and feel it was because
of me. Yes, I believe she loved me but didn't know how to show that
love because of her own past and upbringing. Yes, I believe life is
what you make it. You can change or be changed. You can allow life's
circumstances to change you, or you can change life's circumstances.
The choice is ours. We are all different. God did not make two people alike. We may have things in common with another person, but
our DNA is different. We are fearfully and wonderfully made; therefore, we are all unique, created with a purpose to fulfill. But today,
my mother is my greatest support and strength. She supports my
ministry and is always there when I need to be encouraged. She is a
woman of prayer, wisdom, strength, and great faith. She is a woman
of "change."

My Process for Purpose

*Yet, O Lord, You are our father, we are the clay, and You
our potter, and we all are the work of Your hand.*
—Isaiah 64:8, AMP

I am literally at a point in my life and walk with God where I am
being processed by him that I literally don't completely understand.
He took me from one place where everything dried up and brought
me to the wilderness—no family, no friends, just me and God. I
thought in my mind that when God transitioned me, every promise
and blessing would start manifesting immediately. Even this transition was dry. Now I began to question God after being told "Your
steps are ordered by the Lord," "You are not by yourself," "The steps
that you are making right now are steps that are going to get you into
the new path God has constructed for you," "A lot of times, stopping
places are making places," "Favor is going to be on you," etc. Have
you ever been to a place where you have used up all your resources
and all you have left to depend on is God? Only thing you can hope
for is a miracle, an answer, a wind.

Sometimes we may even begin to question God when we are in
a place in our lives that is the total opposite of what God said. We
question God when we begin to feel displaced and uncomfortable
because we are in unfamiliar territory. We have, at times, become so
comfortable in certain areas of our life that when God wants to move
us to a place called better, doubt steps in. If we allow doubt to creep
in, it will begin to manifest and become a part of us to the point that
we lose sight of who we are. Doubt can become the dictate of our

lives if we let it. But I think I got it now! God had to take me away from everything I was familiar with (people, places, things) so that I can receive that which is unfamiliar.

Forgiveness

To the Lord our God belong mercies and forgivenesses,
though we have rebelled against him
—Daniel 9:9, KJV

One of the keys to change is forgiveness. We have to move past unforgiveness so we can begin to be healed from the inside out, and then the process of deliverance will take place.

I found that forgiving myself was one of the hardest things I had to do. To date, I had a daughter twelve years ago, and it was just several years ago that I truly forgave myself for getting involved with someone outside of what I believed and falling into the sin of fornication and adultery, not knowing he was still married. To keep it real, he was only not saved, but he was not thinking about Jesus. After my daughter was born, I spent years wishing her biological father was not her father. I went through my pregnancy by myself and endured to the end.

For those of you who are thinking about becoming sexually involved with someone you are not married to, think twice. Believe me when I tell you there are consequences to sin—not just fornication. But when you are outside the will of God, the consequences can be detrimental. It hinders you from reaching the place in God you should be, and you risk the chance of losing sight of who you are and asking yourself the question, do I really know God? Just like there is a price for the anointing of God to rest on your life, there is a price to pay for living in sin. You have been saved for so many years, loving and serving God, and then you fall into a season of sin. Yes, it was a season, and a very short one, because the enemy made it seem like it was going to be a lifetime commitment. When that season is over, when you come out, God has to take you through another process, a process of deliverance, again. The process can be painful, but I am here to tell you it is all worth it in the end. I went through a lot of lonely nights. I shed many tears. I was depressed and didn't eat some days. I even felt like committing suicide because I felt like I failed not only myself but also God. When I made the decision to keep the child when her biological father was no longer in the picture, I knew that I had to make a decision that would affect not only my life but my daughter's life as well. Until this day, I know I made the right decision to keep my child. She is a smart, vibrant young girl growing up to be a beautiful young woman. She has blessed my life in more ways than I can describe. She is gifted, talented, loving, giving, compassionate, and caring—all the characteristics a mother can ever ask for in a child.

If you want to be used by God, go through your process. Let God do his work in you, and I am a living witness you will be grateful in the end. God wants clean vessels. He wants to purge us from all filthiness and anything that is in us that does not please him. Our ultimate goal should be to live a life that is pleasing to God (Hebrews 11:5).

Learning to love myself made room for me to genuinely love others. The Holy Spirit had to teach me how to love right. Coming to a place of knowing God taught me what unconditional love truly is. No matter what someone has done to us to hurt us, we still must love them no matter what. That in itself is a process that I had to go through, and I didn't want it to be hard, so I gave all my past hurts, unforgiveness, bitterness, hatred, envy, low self-esteem, resentments, and regrets to God in prayer. It seemed like the more I prayed for those that hurt me, the more I could forgive them and love them. I am not saying that I don't struggle in these areas at times, because I still have areas in my life that the Lord is still working on and there are things that I have to recheck, because I need "spot cleaning" from time to time. If we submit to the will of God, he will constantly work on us, constantly cleansing us, constantly sanctifying us. The key to this constant work in us is obedience and submission and having the faith to believe that in and through Christ, being made whole and complete is possible.

Self-Denial

Then said Jesus unto His disciples, if any man will come after me, let him deny himself, and take up his cross and follow me.
—Matthew 16:24

Flesh: I had to allow God to kill it before it killed me. Through every wilderness, there were benefits for my soul (Romans 7:18; 8:13). The soul must decide whether it is to obey the spirit and therefore be united with God and his will or yield to the body (flesh) and all its temptations. Genesis 6:3 says, "And the Lord said, 'My spirit shall not always strive with man, for that he also is flesh, yet his days shall be an hundred and twenty years.'"

Self-denial is giving up what I want and desire to obtain what I need and what God designed for me to have—in other words, letting go of our wants to receive what we need. It's no more me that lives but the Christ that lives in me.

Through It All I Live

I shall live and not die, and declare the works of the Lord.
—Psalms 118:17

"You shall live and not die"—these were the words the spirit of the Lord spoke when the Lord led me on an extended fast after taking seizure medication for many years.

I started having seizures when I was around sixteen years old. Doctors could never determine what was causing me to have seizures. It could have been a number of things, but nothing was conclusive. I went through so many tests, from sleep deprivation to doctors experimenting with different medications, some of which would cause me to have more seizures than I originally was having. I went through CAT scans, EEGs, and MRIs throughout the early part of my life. Eventually, after years of testing, they discovered I had an aneurism on the right frontal lobe of my brain. I had to have brain surgery to remove it; otherwise, I would continue to have seizures. This can cause damage to the brain.

> *According to research it is known that prolonged seizure activity to the brain can cause brain dysfunction therefore leading to cognitive impairment. (American Journal of Neuroradiology, "The Status of Status: Seizures Are Bad for Your Brain's Health," Richard A. Bronen, MD, Yale University School of Medicine New Haven, CT)*

The doctors tried different seizure medications and dosages to see which one would best control the seizures. Eventually, they concluded that Tegretol worked best in controlling my seizures. I was taking up to 2000 mg per day, but after the surgery, the doctors began to slowly lower the dosages.

Years later, when I rededicated my life back to God, the spirit of the Lord spoke to me and told me I would not be on medication for the rest of my life. After I had surgery, I still had to continue the medication or else, the doctors said, I would regress and start having grand malseizures again. There would be times I would experience petite malseizures in which I would stare off and not be able to respond even though I was aware of my surroundings. I can't recall having grand malseizures after having the aneurism removed. Having seizures caused many problems in my daily life. Work became a problem because I worked for transit as a token-booth clerk, and I would have petite malseizures in the midst of doing a transaction. People would call me crazy because all I would do is go into a state of unresponsiveness and stare. I cried many days and nights because people that didn't know of my sickness treated me differently, and at times, I felt that same way when around family members. I could be walking across the street, and suddenly, I would have a petite malseizure and just stop in the middle of the street and couldn't move. I recall a time I was with a friend, walking down the street, and I had a grand malseizure, and she was screaming, asking people for help, and no one stopped to help. All I can remember is falling to the ground and us ending up in the Housing Authority police station across where I had the seizure.

I was diagnosed at age thirteen as a carrier of hepatitis B. As some may know, hepatitis B can be contracted by having unprotected sex with a person infected with the virus, body piercing with unsterilized instruments, personal items of an infected person such as a toothbrush or a razor, or a mother can pass it on to her baby during delivery

As years passed, I developed chronic hepatitis B, which is a virus that can cause damage to the liver. I went through a number of liver biopsies and was prescribed medication that caused side effects, so

I eventually discontinued taking it. I experienced abdominal pain and chronic fatigue to the point where I couldn't at times get out of the bed; I was constantly sick. I can remember going to Bible class sick and the instructor telling me to go home because I could barely make it through the class. But today as I penned these words in the book, God has healed me of hepatitis B, and my blood panels confirmed lower numbers when tested. I currently only go for follow-up appointments once a year. God is my Jehovah Rapha, the Lord, my healer. You just have to trust and believe God as you walk in faith and obedience. I can go on and on about how God has healed my body time and time again from many things. I can truly say that because of God's loving kindness and mercy toward me, he has forgiven all my iniquities, healed all my diseases, and redeemed my life from destruction (Psalms 103:3, 4).

Prophetic Words of Encouragement and Impartation

There are times in our lives that we feel discouraged, hurt, broken and want to give up and feel like no one cares. Today I want to let you know that through every trial, every disappointment, and all the rejection, you may have to endure that God will speak a word in your life to encourage you, help strengthen you, bring deliverance in your life, and let you know there is still hope. Sometimes you may have to revisit those words to remind you of what God promised what he is about to do not only in your life but also in the body of Christ. It is so important that you are in the place to receive from the Lord and not become displaced by life circumstances. Going to that place to receive from God may mean going before the Lord for yourself to hear what he is saying to you personally. You just have to continue to trust God and believe that if he said it, it shall come to pass. Just believe. For those that need to know that God, as well as the body of Christ, is still moving in your lives, here are some words from the Lord that I want to share with you.

Penned November 17, 2011, from my monthly newsletter, the *Prophetic Voice*:

Position Yourself For the Shift

"...Not by might, nor by power, but by my spirit, saith the Lord of hosts." Zechariah 4:6

Expository Scripture: Ephesians 4

The book of Ephesians contains divine nuggets of the revelation of Christ and God's ultimate plan and goal for the church. This letter unleashes the epitome of all the ingredients needed to help us grow into a body that christ intended for us. In the book of Ephesians chapter 4, Pauls tells us that we are to make an earnest attempt to "keep the unity of the Spirit in the bond of peace", and that God "gave gifts unto men". He also gives us exhortations concerning the christian life, how christians should walk worthy of their calling, and preserving the unity of the Spirit through love and not "walk as the Gentiles" but as those who are new creatures in Christ.

The ministry gifts are Christ's provison for the church; to build up, edify and mature the saints. In Ephesians 4 verse 8 ["When he ascended up on high, he led captivity captive, and gave gifts unto men"] tells us when these gifts were given and verse 12 ["For the perfecting of the saints for the work of the ministry, for the edifying of the body of Christ"] gives us the purpose of the ministry gifts. This chapter also gives us the ultimate goal of the ministry gifts; to become one in the faith, have the true knowledge of the Son of God and become spiritually mature christians no more being children tossed to and fro believing eveything we see and hear, and then concur that it is God. For we are to not believe every spirit but, try the spirit to see if they be of God and speak the truth in love.

We are living in a time where there are false teachers, false prophets, and false apostles (2 Cor. 11:13–14, 1 Peter 2:1). A spirit of deception has infiltrated the church to the point where there is no genuine discernment (Luke 21:8, Ephesians 5:6–7). The love of many is and has waxed cold (Mat. 24:12). There is a lack of prayer, and fasting has become foreign to many. Many are not feeding their spirit with the word of God (Luke 4:4, Eph. 6:17), but are feeding it with more and more carnality that we have become comfortable in a state of being carnal; saying anything and doing anything, especially in the house of God. Many of us are not spirit filled but flesh filled. Our temples are defiled and God is calling the church to a heartfelt repentance of godly sorrow (Joel 2:12–13). We want revival, but true revival can't come unless we repent and turn from our wicked ways (2 Chron. 7:14). God is calling his church to repentance so the church can be established the way he intended for it to be (Acts 16:4–5, Hebrews 8:6–13). The wrath and judgement of God will fall on many because of their hardened hearts (Romans 1:18, 1 Peter 4:17, Jeremiah 33:14, 2 Cor. 5:10). God is calling us to holiness (Lev. 11:44, 1 Cor. 3:17, 1 Thess. 4:7).

God is re-establishing divine order in the body of Christ. At this time and season there is great warfare in the body of Christ. This is the time when God's intecessory prayer warriors must band together in the spirit and war. We have to develop a relentless prayer and fast life. These two coupled together will enable us to discern and see what is happening in the realm of the spirit so that we can pray effectively. You see, when we are active participants in the natural shift then a divine shift takes place.

God has a remnant that He is about to raise up, and if you are part of that remnant you have to position yourself (Romans 9:27, Jeremiah 23:1–4). How do we position ourself? First, we must be in a place where we know the voice of God and know what he is saying to us (John 10:27). We are living in a time when the foundational establishment of the church must be purged and restructured. Many in leadership have taken on a spirit of rebellion and pride. Therefore, leadership has to be dismembered and reestablished, because the anointing flows from the head down (Lev. 8:12, Psalms 133:1–2). It is going to take the anointing of God to destroy the yokes. God is preparing and about raise up his apostles, prophets and prophetesses in the end times, and these vessels will be used of the Lord to see that God's purpose is fulfilled in the earth and prepare the church for the coming of the Lord. This is why the warfare is so great for those who have a prophetic mantle on their lives. Attacks from the enemy will increase, therefore God will equip these vessels with spiritual weapons. The prophets ministry is designed by God to help protect the church from the devices and plans of the enemy. They have to be the watchmen in the church. They must Shamar (Hebrew word meaning protect and watch) the church. Watching and praying, always watching and praying, not coming down from the wall. The end time church must be built with all five ministry gifts in operation. A spirit of dillusion has clouded the minds of many. Witchcraft (pride, no respect for authority, lack of submission, etc.) is coming in at full speed because many people of God fail to submit themselves to the will of God, therefore giving the enemy free access. Man is being glorified and not God. Many are operating in gifts from old residue, because they fail to seek the Lord for a "fresh word" and the anointing of God is not present, but many operate under a "counterfeit" anointing (Revelation 2:18–29). Many say they are children of God, but don't have "the power" to live holy, therefore sin is on the rampage in the body of Christ (2 Timothy 3:5).

Throughout history God's chosen ["many are called few are chosen"]people have experienced insurmountable difficulties when trying to carry out the purpose of God. Obstacles are permitted by God as a test of faith in which we have to trust God and the power of his spirit. A perfect example of this is when Zerrubbabel (Ezra 3:8–13, 4:3–4; Zechariah 4:9) was given the task of rebuilding the house of the Lord. From the beginning the adversary had "weakened the hands of the people and troubled them in building", but because of God's divine intervention, and their commitment to the task they were able to restore the temple. The Lord had declared out of the mouth of his prophet, "The hand of Zerubbabel have laid the foundation of this house; his hands shall also finish it..." What we must continue to see and understand is that, God will provide the resources needed to get the work done.

The exercise of a living faith means an increase of spiritual strength and development of trust in God. Human power and human might did not establish the church of God, and neither can it destroy it. The church was established on a sure foundation, which is Jesus Christ our rock, and the gates of hell shall not and will not prevail against it. We have to mount up with wings as eagles, continue to run and not be weary, walk and not faint.

Penned on December 9, 2015

There is about to be a "birthing in the earth" Earth prophetically representing us. We were created from the dust of the earth and we all have a spiritual womb (the human spirit), where the things of God are birthed out. God makes deposits in the "earth". God is processing us for the manifestation of the blessings He has promised. In order for a birthing to take place there is pain (trials), a "shaking" in the spirit, and testing of faith. In the natural when a woman is impregnated, she finds herself going through different stages in her pregnancy that are sometime uncomfortable or even unbearable. In the spirit, the conception and development of purpose, promise, restoration, deliverance, and so forth is a process of time when that thing has to ripen and mature to be able to come forth (in the natural this is gestation). At the time of delivery (the manifestation of what you are impregnated with in the spirit), the preliminary experiences or stages of preparation are what qualifies us to bring forth that thing and can resemble the labor contractions a woman has when giving birth. Our trials, test, believing and trusting God, etc. are the tools of preparation for what God has promised us, called us to do and His purpose and plan for our life to be fulfilled. When there is a quaking in our spirit (trials, test of faith, and so forth) we can be assured that there is going to be a great releasing of power, change/transformation, restoration and deliverance coming forth. Just like the womb or birth canal has to be opened when giving birth so does our spirit have to be open to receive from God, and this to can be painful because we are stretched beyond our normal capacity. So we just have to continue to walk by faith, wait on the Lord, trust in Him only, and know that everything He promised it shall come to pass. Hold on, the wait is almost over!!!

Penned March 2, 2016

A Word from the Lord:

I hear you says the Lord. I want your worship. Worship me says the Lord. It's in your worship that I will release my promises. It's in your worship that I will release my miracles. It's in your worship, I will take you not just to another level in me, but another dimension. A place you have never experienced before. A place where you have never been before. A new place. A place of refreshing, a place of promise. A new place, a place of my glory. You will walk in my glory. You will pray in my glory. Guard your eye gates for this too I will impart my glory. Guard your ear gates for this too I will impart my glory. When others look on you, they will not see you, but they will see the manifestation of my glory resting on you saith the spirit of truth. I will begin to download in your spirit new ideas. I hear the Lord say everything new. Nothing old. Walk in faith and obedience. Guard and protect the place where I'm about to take you says the Lord.

My prayer is that this book has blessed you, brought perspective into your life and opened the door to deliverance for your life. Remember there is hope, because you have purpose and you are purpose!

References

The Holy Spirit

The American Heritage College Dictionary, 4th ed. Boston, NY: Houghton Mifflin Company.

Trimm, Cindy. *Binding the Strong Man.* (2005). Ft. Lauderdale, FL: Kingdom Life Publishing.

Strong, James. *The New Strong's Complete Dictionary of Bible Words.* (1996). Thomas Nelson Publishers.

Miller, Betty. *Pride and Beauty: A Snare.* Bibleresources.org/pride.

Wiersbe, Warren W. *The Strategy of Satan: How to Detect and Defeat Him.* (1979). Carol Stream, Illinois: Tyndale House Publishers Inc.

Ells, Alfred H. *Unmasking Hidden Pride.* Counselor's Corner, Volume II, Issue II. Counselor's Corner.

Peacocke, Dennis. *You Got to Be Wrong in order to Get Right.* Bibleresources.org/pride.

Price, Paula A. *The Prophet's Handbook: A Guide to Prophecy and Its Operation.* New Kensington, PA: Whitaker House.

Price, Paula A. *The Prophet's Dictionary: The Ultimate Guide to Supernatural Wisdom.* New Kensington, PA: Whitaker House.

The Names of God Bible. God's Word Translation. Grand Rapids, MI: Baker's Publishing Group.

Matthew Henry's Commentary on the Whole Bible. Hendricks Publishers Inc.

Nee, Watchman. *The Spiritual Man.* Richmond, Virginia: Christian Fellowship Publishers.

Holy Bible. New Living Translation. Carol Stream, Illinois: Tyndale House Publishers Inc.

Life in the Spirit Study Bible. King James Version. Grand Rapids, Michigan: Zondervan.

Amplified Bible Parallel Edition. King James Version. Zondervan Publishing House.

(http://www.webmd.com/hepatitis/hepb-guide/hepatitis-b-topic-overview).

About the Author

Stephanie Arrington is a born native of New York City. She currently resides in North Carolina with her daughter. She is a loving mother and grandmother. She holds a BA in psychology and an MS in general and special education. As a dedicated student committed to the Word of God, she received certificates of recognition for her diligence and excellent attendance and an Award of Merit for Achieving Highest Honors for outstanding academic achievement and excellence in the study of God's word. She was ordained a missionary on May 22, 2011. She is a prophetic intercessor and prayer warrior gifted with a strong prayer mantle and prophetic call. At Salvation and Deliverance Church, where the late Apostle William Brown was the founder and overseer, she served as a prayer warrior for over fifteen years on the prayer team, under the leadership of Mother Betty Williams. Thereafter, she transitioned under the prophetic teaching and tutelage of Apostle Andre Cook, pastor of Life Chapel West in Hollis, NY and founder and overseer of Kingdom Life Fellowship of Churches. In April 2016, she came under the mentorship of Dr. Jonathan I. Shaw Sr. who is the senior pastor of Crown Ministries International Inc. in Brooklyn, NY as part of The Pashat Exchange Mentorship Program which she completed. She is the founder and CEO of PPV Ministries, Inc. (Prayer, Purpose & Vision Ministries) and formed the Prophetic Voice: Warriors and Intercessors prayer group. She has delivered the word of God in different capacities. She believes in living a life of obedience, discipline, holiness, and submission to the Holy Spirit.

CPSIA information can be obtained
at www.ICGtesting.com
Printed in the USA
LVHW030703170522
718962LV00001B/134